NEW ORLEANS
·COFFEE·

NEW ORLEANS
·COFFEE·

A Rich History

SUZANNE STONE

With Contributions from David Feldman

AMERICAN PALATE

Published by American Palate
A Division of The History Press
Charleston, SC
www.historypress.com

Copyright © 2019 by Suzanne Stone
All rights reserved

First published 2019

Manufactured in the United States

ISBN 9781467141390

Library of Congress Control Number: 2019937039

Notice: The information in this book is true and complete to the best of our knowledge. It is offered without guarantee on the part of the author or The History Press. The author and The History Press disclaim all liability in connection with the use of this book.

All rights reserved. No part of this book may be reproduced or transmitted in any form whatsoever without prior written permission from the publisher except in the case of brief quotations embodied in critical articles and reviews.

This book is dedicated to my family:

*Miriam Kramer and Jared Cooper
Adam Kramer and Molly Kramer
John Ford Kramer and Sidney Justin Kramer*

CONTENTS

List of Recipes	9
Acknowledgements	11
1. The Special Flavor of New Orleans	13
2. From Kaldi to the Crescent City	19
3. Creole Coffee: Like the Benediction that Follows after Prayer	33
Queens of Creole Cooking	39
4. The Dawn of American New Orleans: Antebellum Markets	43
5. Coffee at Home	57
6. Chicory	65
7. The Golden Era of New Orleans	73
8. New Orleans Rises Again	85
9. Shops in the French Market	101
10. Beyond the French Market	113
11. Coffee's Three Waves	121
12. Coffee in New Orleans Today	129
New Orleans' Coffee Women	170
Bibliography	175
Index	189
About the Author	192

RECIPES

Breakfast Sausage Spice Cake	32
Memere's Pralines	38
Angela's Microwave Pralines	38
Dairy- and Gluten-Free Coffee Granola	54
Coffee and Chicory Cookies	71
Coffee-Roasted Sweet Potato Dessert Fries Drizzled with Dark Chocolate	82
Honey Cake	99
Coffee Cream Filling for Cream Puffs	111
Glazes and Sauces for Ham, Chicken and Beef	119
White Alligator	139
Midnight on the Bayou™	140

ACKNOWLEDGEMENTS

There are so many people to acknowledge. Linda Anderson, whom I met while volunteering at the World War II Museum, introduced me to Libby Bollino, owner of Lucky Bean Tours and master storyteller. Libby hired me early in my career as a tour guide and gave me the opportunity to write a blog for Lucky Bean. An editor at The History Press saw a short item I wrote on Old Rose and Henry Lonsdale and invited me to write this book. Thanks to David Feldman, because without his agreeing to be part of this adventure, I would not have taken it on. David and I met during training with the Friends of the Cabildo, where we were told that, along with learning New Orleans history and honing storytelling skills, we would make future best friends. Every part of this book has been improved with David's help.

I am pleased to acknowledge the other tour guides who love New Orleans and its history and are committed to accurate storytelling, especially those who read early drafts of different chapters and improved them: Tish Casey, Richard Crawford, Marcia Curole and Lynn Frank. Also, thanks to Ben Crowe, who provided a valuable book about 1890s New Orleans, and Jeannine Chance, who introduced me to Phyllis Jordan. This book could not have happened without the many people David and I interviewed. Rien Fertel and Mary Gehman, in particular, offered assistance in the beginning and helped steer me through the shoals of two of the stories that had originally piqued my interest in coffee in New Orleans: chicory and Old Rose.

Acknowledgements

Thanks also to my friends, especially Pam Jones, who was the first copyeditor of early chapters and warned me of bad habits I tried to avoid thereafter; Kat Kay, who was always available to encourage me and spur me on during dry spells of writer's block; Simone Duhon, with her cheerful words and tremendous interest; and Carolyn Lenz, for her knowledge of New Orleans and introduction to Leah Chase. I have always considered librarians the best people around, and those at the Mid-City branch of the New Orleans Library, at Tulane University and at the Historic New Orleans Collection all lived up to that appellation and provided as much enthusiasm and encouragement as help.

The editors at The History Press took me under their wings and guided me through every step in the process, almost seed to cup, as those in the coffee industry would say. I have come to know so many people in that industry and am impressed with the genuine niceness of each person. Everyone was eager to participate and share their stories, insights, hopes, dreams and memories.

I am also indebted to the tour companies I work for. In addition to Lucky Bean, they are Ghost City Tours, Tastebud Tours (a great way to whet one's appetite for New Orleans culinary history), Nola Tour Guy and Two Chicks Walking Tours. A last shout-out goes to all those coffee shops in the city that always welcome tour guides.

1
THE SPECIAL FLAVOR OF NEW ORLEANS

Today, Latin America leads the world in the production of coffee, and America is the largest consumer. New Orleans lies in the middle of that profitable configuration.
—Louise McKinney

New Orleans is unlike any other city anywhere else; like the local coffee, a dark roast flavored more or less discreetly with chicory, it has its special flavor, and the visitor is aware of it immediately.
—Oliver Evans

Coffee runs through the history of New Orleans like the Mississippi River runs through the city itself. This is the story of the three-hundred-year love affair New Orleans has had with coffee. It all began around 1720 when Gabriel Mathieu de Clieu stole a cutting from a coffee tree in King Louis XV's Royal Garden in Versailles. He protected and nurtured the cutting on the perilous voyage across the Atlantic and planted it in French Martinique. Eventually, 90 percent of the world's coffee descended from that one tree, including much that made its way into New Orleans.

New Orleans was founded in 1718 by Jean Baptiste Le Moyne, *sieur* (short for *monsieur*, which once was an honorific title for royalty) de Bienville. He was not the first European on the Lower Mississippi. The Spaniard Hernando de Soto crossed the river in 1542 at a place in what is now Arkansas. By the time the French-Canadian fur trader René-Robert Cavelier, sieur de La

Gabriel-Mathieu Francois de Clieu. European Coffee History Engraving. *From Wikimedia Commons.*

Salle, first sailed down the river 140 years later, the indigenous population had been largely destroyed by disease. On April 9, 1682, at the mouth of the river, La Salle and his retinue of priests erected a cross, performed mass before the assembled native peoples and buried a lead tablet engraved with a cross and the coat of arms of the king. The tablet, inscribed in Latin, claimed the river and all the land drained by it for King Louis XIV. The land La Salle called La Louisiane, "Land of Louis," encompassed the river and its drainage basin.

La Salle had no idea of what he had claimed for King Louis XIV, nor was the king interested in the more than one million square miles from present-day upstate New York to western Montana, from Canada south to the Gulf of Mexico. Countless streams and 154 navigable rivers feed the Mississippi. Fourteen thousand miles of navigable waterways would become a vital water highway system from the Appalachian Mountains to the Rocky Mountains and from Canada to the Gulf of Mexico.

By the end of the seventeenth century, though, England and Spain were very interested in France's claim. In 1699, the French king sent an expedition to establish a permanent presence in southern Louisiana. It was led by French-Canadian naval officers Pierre LeMoyne, sieur d'Iberville, and his younger brother, Jean Baptiste, sieur de Bienville. They established settlements along the Gulf Coast at Mobile, Biloxi and Ocean Springs. They also built several forts upriver.

Iberville died of yellow fever in 1706, leaving twenty-four-year old Bienville in charge. In 1718, he and his small group of kinsmen, concessionaires, soldiers, indentured workmen and prisoners cut the first cane breaks for a new settlement. Bienville chose the highest piece of ground nearest the mouth of the Mississippi River.

A Rich History

The land de La Salle called La Louisiane encompassed the river and its drainage basin, including rivers as far as the Alleghenies to the east and the Rockies to the west. *Licensed under the Creative Commons Attribution-Share Alike 3.0.*

It was ninety miles to the mouth of the river and about eight to ten feet above sea level at its highest point. Also, there was a back door into the site to the Gulf of Mexico from Lake Pontchartrain by way of Bayou Saint John, a finger of water that cut deeply into the city. This site was situated on a curve between two sharp bends in the river, making it easily defensible against attacking ships. Bienville called it the "beautiful crescent," which provided an early nickname for New Orleans: the Crescent City. He called the settlement "La Nouvelle Orleans" for his patron, the Duke of Orleans. Since King Louis XV was a child, Orleans ruled as regent.

As Louise McKinney said, the founders "chose the present site for New Orleans (precarious though it is, built on alluvial silt washed from the Missouri and Ohio rivers and more than 250 other tributaries) precisely because they recognized its strategic geographic importance as a gateway to the riches of North America."

The Louisiana colony and the nascent city of New Orleans faced a serious problem from the outset: very few people came to settle. The Company

Jean Baptiste Le Moyne, sieur de Bienville, founder of New Orleans. *From Wikimedia Commons.*

of the West, whose publicly traded stock gyrated frenetically on the Paris market, was granted a thirty-year concession to develop Louisiana. In return, the company promised to entice six thousand whites to Louisiana and bring nine thousand Africans to be enslaved there. The first two ships bringing Africans arrived in 1719 from Senegambia. About two thousand German Catholics fleeing the calamities war and bad weather had visited upon their native Alsace fell prey to the Company of the West's false advertising and emigrated. They moved upriver from the city and settled as farmers, bakers, butchers and brewers. Some well-connected French were granted land concessions above and below the city. They grew indigo and later tobacco, cotton and sugar.

Absenting volunteers to Louisiana, the Duke d'Orleans instructed his police and soldiers to round up all the undesirables they could find and transport them to the coast of France to be sent to Louisiana. These thieves, smugglers, beggars and prostitutes constituted much of New Orleans's founding generation. While they were more accustomed to taking what they needed rather than making or growing it, they were able to start producing new French citizens. The Company of the West failed in 1720 without fulfilling any of its promises. The financial bubble in Paris burst. Supply ships from France became more infrequent in New Orleans. By 1730, France had all but completely lost interest in Louisiana.

Early New Orleans was a little rough around the edges, to say the least. Bienville requested that nuns be sent to the city to staff the hospital and educate rich, white girls. Among the Ursuline nuns who arrived in 1726 was the young Marie Hachard, who wrote back to France, "The Devil has a very strong empire…but that does not take away from us the hope of destroying him, with God's love." To aid in that enterprise, the first public executioner was appointed. A deal was struck with the enslaved Louis Congo. He would serve as the executioner in exchange for his freedom, a land grant, compensation and release from service for his wife. He was paid according to the punishment. A simple hanging paid less than breaking on the wheel or drawing and quartering. Punishments were carried out in the public square in front of the church before large crowds.

The early settlers found the land and subtropical climate different from their previous homes. Among many other differences, their usual foods were not at hand; they learned about new foods and drinks and substitutes for their favorites from the indigenous people and the people they brought from Africa to enslave. Bienville, who maintained generally good relations with the native tribes, sent settlers and slaves to live with the native peoples to stave off starvation. They taught the settlers to grow what are known as the "Three Sisters": corn, beans and squash. The enslaved Africans brought rice and okra with them. The bread-loving French found that wheat wouldn't grow around New Orleans, so bread was made from corn and rice. The native peoples also introduced the settlers to an intoxicating drink made of fermented fruits and berries, ratafia. The Germans brewed beer. Bear was a substitute for the accustomed meat.

Coffee, however, was available. By the 1730s, coffee trees had been introduced into the French colony of Saint-Domingue. French Saint-Domingue became the most lucrative colony in the world, producing as much as 60 percent of the coffee and 40 percent of the sugar consumed in Europe. Tobacco and cocoa were also grown and exported. France had a corner on the addiction market in the eighteenth century. But that wealth came at a heavy cost. The more than 500,000 enslaved people lived and worked under particularly brutal conditions on the coffee and sugar cane plantations. The entire population of enslaved people had to be replenished every twenty years. But, the world's appetite for coffee, tobacco and cocoa was and is insatiable.

All was not bleak during the first four decades. The wealthier early settlers did quite well under the faraway, laissez-faire administration of the French. Those who could afford it enjoyed fancy clothes, good food, fine wine, music, dancing and gambling. A roulette wheel is said to have come with the first ship. The others made do with makeshift taverns; public drunkenness has always been a problem in New Orleans. As for coffee, the enslaved Africans drank brews made of ground nuts, roots and dried sweet potatoes. We can only surmise that the wealthier French, at least, enjoyed expensive coffee brought on ships, which often stopped in Saint-Domingue before continuing on to New Orleans.

Spain acquired Louisiana in 1762. The French were losing the French and Indian War to the British. France lost the eastern half of the Louisiana Territory and the maritime provinces of Canada known as Acadia. To avoid losing the rest of Louisiana to the British, the Bourbon king of France ceded New Orleans and the Louisiana Territory to the west of the Mississippi to his Bourbon cousin, the King of Spain, via the secret Treaty of Fontainebleau. France had never seen a profit from Louisiana, and the Spanish saw the land not necessarily as a profitable colony but as a buffer between the British, who now were close to Spain's silver mines in Mexico.

The Spanish were competent, conscientious and professional administrators. They made many infrastructure improvements, including streetlights and sanitation regulations. They established the first police and fire protection and instituted price controls in the filthy public food markets. They spent millions rebuilding after the fires of 1788 and 1794. The Spanish brought in more Africans, largely from the Congo. They encouraged immigration from Ireland and the Canary Islands, as well as accepted and resettled some six thousand French Catholic Acadians expelled by the British. The Acadians moved to Southwest Louisiana, where they could maintain their language and culture, living as they had before as fishers and trappers. Over time, they became known as Cajuns.

Between 1791 and 1804, the enslaved people of Saint-Domingue led and won a revolution, leading to the establishment of Haiti. At the end of the Spanish period, the city began to welcome its first refugees from unrest in Saint-Domingue. Spanish rule unofficially came to an end in 1800 when Napoleon took back Louisiana. His plan was to use Louisiana as the food supplier for Saint-Domingue after he reconquered it.

By the time Thomas Jefferson first started dreaming of acquiring New Orleans as the gateway to the vast heartland of the United States, it was a multicultural, multiracial and multilingual city unlike the rest of the United States. That flavor remains the essence of New Orleans.

During the city's three-hundred-year history, enslaved Africans, immigrants and refugees have made their way to New Orleans: French, Senegambians, Spanish, Congolese, Germans, Irish, Italians, Portuguese, Jews, Greeks, Dalmatians, Slavonians, Croatians, Albanian-Sicilian, Lebanese, Filipinos, Chinese, Koreans, Vietnamese, Japanese, Indians. They brought their coffee culture with them and blended it into the *tout ensemble* that is New Orleans.

2

FROM KALDI TO THE CRESCENT CITY

The word *coffee* has roots in several languages. In Yemen, it was called *qahwah*, which originally was a word for wine. It also is thought to be named for the Kaffa region of Ethiopia. Or, it is derived from *quwwa*, Arabic for "power." Some suggest a source in *kafta*, the drink made from the khat plant; both are strong stimulants. From whichever source, in Turkey, the drink was known as *kahveh*, *koffie* in the Netherlands and finally *coffee* in English.

According to legend, coffee was discovered by accident, by an observant goat herder named Kaldi (or Khalid) in the ninth century in Abyssinia (today's Ethiopia). He noticed that goats who nibbled the red cherries of a bush were quite energetic; Morton Satin imagines the goats "were gaily gamboling around, butting heads and pronking about like young gazelles." According to this story, Kaldi then tried the cherries, was equally energetic and then told the abbot of a nearby monastery. The abbot, thinking the cherries were wicked, tossed them into a fire. The aroma of roasting coffee beans changed the abbot's mind, and he then made an infusion for the monks to drink.

From this point on, devil's drink or elixir of the gods—whichever view won out—would determine coffee's future.

The first writings about coffee are by ninth-century Persian physician Abu Bakr Muhammad Ibn Zakariya Ar-Razi, or Rhazes, and tenth-century Persian physician Avicenna, who wrote that coffee—which he says originated in Yemen—was "hot and dry and good for the stomach." Next, according to

Kaldi dancing with his goats. *Drawing by Miriam Kramer.*

William Ukers, came thirteenth-century Sheikh Omar, who first was known for his ability to cure the sick through prayer. When exiled from Mocha (in Yemen, today) to a desert cave, Omar was starving and discovered coffee cherries. He chewed them, roasted them and finally boiled them to obtain a "savory and perfumed drink" that cured his malaise. On his return to Mocha, he was declared a hero for discovery of this "miracle drug."

During the 1300s, the area around Mocha popularized the coffee drink—now made by roasting the cherries, grinding them with a mortar and pestle and then boiling or steeping them in water. Again, a learned cleric endorsed coffee as a health aid. Sheikh Gemaleddin, mufti of Aden, discovered coffee's beneficial effects on his illness and headaches. With this commendation, coffee cultivation and drinking spread throughout Yemen and the rest of the Arab world. In 1517, Sultan Selim I brought coffee to Constantinople, with coffeehouses opening in 1554. These coffeehouses, called "schools of the wise," served residents, as well as merchants and travelers from the known world. They were outfitted as lounges and richly carpeted; in addition to coffee, many forms of entertainment were offered.

Coffee's popularity threatened its continued existence in Muslim lands. About 1570, certain imams noticed the coffeehouses attracted more consumers than mosques did adherents. Surely, they reasoned, coffee must be a sin. Earlier efforts to ban coffee in Egypt that were led by clerics and opposed by physicians were stopped by a justice who employed an experiential method—imbibing coffee and serving it to the warring parties, thus unifying "the contending parties, and [bringing] coffee into greater esteem than ever." A ban was imposed on coffeehouses, resulting in coffee drinking moving into secret "speakeasies." Later, the ban was revoked.

Coffee's path in Europe was similar. It was introduced in Germany (1573) and Italy (1580) by physicians, and Catholic clerics attempted to ban it in 1594. As William Ukers stated, some "priests appealed to Pope Clement VIII (1535–1605) to have [coffee's] use forbidden among Christians, denouncing it as an invention of Satan. They claimed that the Evil One, having forbidden his followers, the infidel Moslems, the use of wine—no doubt because it was sanctified by Christ and used in the Holy Communion—had given them as a substitute this hellish black brew of his which they called coffee. For Christians to drink it was to risk falling into a trap set by Satan for their souls." As in Egypt, experiencing the drink carried the day: the pope allegedly stated, after his first cup of coffee, "Why, this Satan's drink is so delicious that it would be a pity to let the infidels have exclusive use of it. We shall fool Satan by baptizing it and making it a truly Christian beverage."

With that, coffee began its march into the rest of Europe. Both the English and Dutch East India Companies brought coffee from Mocha on the tip of the Arabian Peninsula. Also, trade from North Africa brought coffee. Finally, Turkish armies introduced coffee as they marched into Vienna. Thus, coffee was introduced into Holland (1616), England (1623), Germany (1670), Italy (1650), Vienna (1683) and the rest of Europe. The Ottoman Turks, fleeing the siege of Vienna, left five hundred bags of coffee behind. The Viennese thought the beans were camel feed, but a Pole who had been prisoner of the Ottomans recognized the coffee and introduced it to Vienna.

Marseille merchants are responsible for introducing coffee to France. First was Pierre de la Roque, in 1644. Within twenty years, several other Marseille merchants with trade in Turkey brought coffee beans home, followed by apothecaries' commercial importation from Egypt. In 1669, a Turkish ambassador visited King Louis XIV, who did not receive him immediately. While waiting to meet with the king, the ambassador entertained the elite of Paris in a Turkish style, including serving coffee. In 1671, the first French coffeehouse opened. Within fifty years of its introduction, coffee was a runaway hit in France. No less a person than François-Marie Arouet, whose pen name was Voltaire, was singing its praises, crediting the drink as his philosophical muse; he supposedly drank between forty and fifty cups a day. In 1682, one Damame François received the sole license to sell coffee for ten years in all of France, including its territories. In 1689, the Café Procope was opened by François Procope, a *limonadier* (lemonade vender) who had a royal license to sell spices, ices, barley water, lemonade and other such refreshments. The first Italian coffee sellers, about forty years earlier, also were lemonade vendors, who sold chocolate and liquor drinks as well.

Coffeehouses had started in England a few years earlier. In 1650, a Lebanese Jew in Oxford named Jacob opened the first coffeehouse in England. This was followed just two years later with the first coffeehouse in London opened by Pasqua Rosée. Others quickly opened. Before this, the only common meeting place was the tavern, where drinks were intoxicating. At a coffeehouse, conversation was encouraged. Opposition soon came from alehouse keepers. The easiest attack was on health. Physicians entered the fray. Already, Dr. William Harvey, who discovered and described human blood circulation, had expressed his preference, not only by drinking coffee profusely throughout his life (1578–1657) but also by leaving at his death fifty-six pounds of coffee to his colleagues at the Royal College of Physicians in London, so they could, as long as possible, gather once a month and "drink a cup in his memory." Harvey had tried coffee as an antidote to drunkenness.

Dr. Thomas Willis, who wrote *Pharmaceutice Rationalis* in 1674, understood that coffee was likely not harmful, at least in moderation, and could provide benefits. He said it could "attack the heart and cause tremblings [*sic*] in the limbs." But, "being daily drunk it wonderfully clears and enlightens each part of the Soul and disperses all the clouds of every Function."

In 1674, before Dr. Willis's advice was widely accepted, a "well-willer" published "The Women's Petition Against Coffee Representing to Publick Consideration the Grand Inconveniencies Accruing to their Sex from the Excessive Use of that Drying, Enfeebling Liquor." The complaint was,

> *The fame in our Apprehensions can consist in nothing more than the brisk* Activity *of our men, who in former Ages were justly esteemed the* Ablest Performers *in Christendom; But to our unspeakable Grief, we find of late a very sensible* Decay *of that true* Old English Vigor; *our Gallants being every way so* Frenchified, *that they are become mere Cock-sparrows, fluttering things that come on Sa sa, with a world of Fury, but are not able to* stand *to it, and in the very first Charge fall down* flat *before us. Never did Men wear greater breeches, or carry less in them of any* Mettle *whatsoever.*... [Men who drink coffee] *come from it with nothing moist but their snotty Noses, nothing* stiffe *but their Joints, nor* standing *but their Ears.*

A Rich History

Historian Steve Pincus maintains that this pamphlet was not written by women, but as satire by those opposing coffeehouses as places of political unrest. And satirists often used the coffeehouse in their writings: the Tories criticizing them and the Whigs using them as models for social reformation.

Interestingly, while women generally were not admitted into English coffeehouses, their presence was known. According to William Ukers, "the London City *Quaeries* for 1660 makes mention of a 'she-coffee merchant.'" He and Markman Ellis both discuss the operations of a number of other female coffeehouse owners. Women also worked in coffeehouses, and Markman Ellis stated that "satirists made much of the flirtatious banter between the male clientele and the female staff."

As in the Middle East, the coffeehouse in Europe became a place for men to gather for intellectual and political conversation and amusements. Another similarity was that some of the conversations could center on radical politics of the day, generally efforts toward democracy and republicanism that were sweeping the continent in the 1700s. Food writer Margaret Visser noted the coffeehouses were egalitarian meeting places where, among other things, "men and women could, without impropriety, consort as they had never done before." They also, due to coffee's ability to keep its drinkers awake and sober, became places of intellectual conversations about arts, science, economics and politics. In England, coffeehouses, which served coffee for one penny a cup and were popular places for discussions of current topics, including politics, were called "penny universities."

In part because of its location, directly opposite the newly opened Comédie Française, the Café Procope became the gathering place of many noted French actors, authors, dramatists and musicians of the eighteenth century. It also attracted the great thinkers and politicians of the day. In 1789, Jean-Paul Marat, Maximilien Robespierre, Jacques Hébert, Georges Danton and other lights of the French Revolution gathered there. In 1790, when Benjamin Franklin died, the coffeehouse went into mourning—with the walls, inside and out, covered in black bunting—to respect the man many in France revered as "the great friend of republicanism."

According to legend, a frequent visitor to Café Procope was a poor young artillery officer who, when not drinking coffee, played chess there. This was Napoléon Bonaparte, who, it is said, had to once leave his hat for security while he went out of the café seeking money to pay his tab. Throughout his life, Napoleon indulged his passion for coffee. It is recorded that he played chess and drank coffee each evening on his voyage to Elba. He also drank

The Emperor Napoleon in his study at the Tuileries. *From Wikimedia Commons.*

coffee on St. Helena. (Coffee plants brought there from Yemen in 1733 were flourishing.)

Every year in France, new cafés opened. At the same time, France was getting involved in coffee cultivation for trade. In 1658, the Dutch cultivated coffee in Ceylon and, in 1699, sent a Yemeni or arabica coffee seedling to Jakarta in Java. The Dutch also grew coffee in Sumatra, Celebes, Timor, Bali and other East Indies islands. In 1711, Holland succeeded in exporting coffee from Java. In 1714, Amsterdam's burgomaster presented King Louis XV with a healthy descendant of the original tree from Java. The king had the plant cultivated in the first greenhouses in Europe at the Palace of Versailles so he could directly source his own coffee beans.

With descendants of this plant, France began cultivating coffee on the island of Île Bourbon (now Réunion), off the east coast of Africa. Then, in 1720, Gabriel Mathieu de Clieu, a young naval officer serving on Martinique, obtained two seedlings from the coffee trees in the Paris Royal Gardens and successfully planted them in Martinique, where they flourished. He distributed beans (the seed of the coffee plant) and was aided in the effort by hurricane winds and rains, which carried the coffee beans to other nearby islands. (Note: in 1752, the Portuguese began coffee cultivation in Brazil, which now accounts for about 25 percent of the world's supply.) According to William Ukers, by 1738, the French had succeeded in transplanting coffee beans for cultivation to Saint-Domingue and the cafés and coffeehouses on that island as well as all French territories, including, no doubt, the small capital of Louisiana. Thus, coffee was an old habit in Louisiana before its introduction in Boston with the 1770 Tea Party, generally considered its first arrival in the United States. And, by 1788, as coffee spread throughout the new world, Saint-Domingue supplied half of the world's coffee, according to Mark Pendergrast.

The Spanish Connection

It is likely that coffee came relatively earlier to Spain, since it was governed by Muslims at various times between 711 and 1492. At some point, the coffee drinkers of Spain developed a roasting method that produces very dark, almost black, oily beans that make strong coffee known as Spanish Roast. Just as the French prefer a dark roast and strong coffee, the Spanish often drink *café con leche* (coffee with milk) at breakfast and strong, black coffee the rest of the day, typically at a morning break, lunchtime and after dinner.

A Brief Coffee Primer
by David Feldman

What images come to mind when you hear "the tropics"? Steamy rainforests, verdant mountainsides, jungles under a dense canopy of trees, monsoons, the Amazon River, the darkest Congo. Perhaps, and more likely, you imagine white sandy beaches under swaying palm trees and crystal-clear turquoise water. Most of us don't have to imagine bananas, avocados, Coke or Pepsi, tea, coffee or chocolate. Coffee, along with sisters tea, cacao and the kola nut, grows in a belt that encircles the earth between the Tropics of Cancer and Capricorn. The year-round temperature is about 64 degrees Fahrenheit. Seasons are either wet or dry.

Coffee is the second-most traded commodity in the world after oil. The world's 8 billion inhabitants consume 4 billion cups of coffee a day. Americans drink just under 2 cups; 400 million per day; 146 billion cups each year. Each coffee-drinking American needs sixteen coffee trees to sate her or his yearly coffee appetite. The United States, though, does not even rank among the

Coffee plantation with shade trees in Orosí, Costa Rica. *Photograph by Dirk van der Made. From Wikimedia Commons. Licensed under the Creative Commons Attribution-1.0 Generic license.*

top twenty countries in per capita coffee consumption. Finland is number one, with Finns consuming fifty-eight pounds of coffee per capita per year.

World coffee production topped 21 billion pounds in 2017, most of it shipped in 132-pound burlap sacks. More than 20 million men, women and children depend on coffee for their livelihoods. They are links in a worldwide coffee chain extending upward from the tree to your artistically decorated latté.

Coffee trees belong to the family Rubiacea, which has 450 genera and around 6,500 species worldwide. The genus *Coffea* includes over 100 species, but the world seems to prefer only 2: *arabica* beans make up 70–75 percent of the world's production, while *robusta* beans, used primarily for instant coffee, makes up the rest. Brazil is the largest supplier of *arabica* beans, and Vietnam is the largest for *robusta* coffee. *Arabica* likes to grow under a canopy of taller trees, at higher elevations with cooler temperatures. *Robusta* is less demanding, can grow at sea level and is simply more robust. *Arabica* is harder and more expensive to cultivate than *robusta*, has a smaller yield, is more susceptible to pests and has half the caffeine

Coffee tree at Kona Coffee Living History Farm. *From Wikimedia Commons.*

(1.5 percent) of *robusta*. Since caffeine is bitter, *robusta* can taste bitter to some drinkers. *Arabica* has more sugar and a much higher concentration of organic compounds, amino acids, which give *arabica* coffees their complex aromas and flavors after roasting. Often, as Mark Pendergrast pointed out, "the rarer the bean, the more expensive and desirable." Thus, Hawaiian Kona and Jamaican Blue Mountain can command higher prices than many coffee connoisseurs believe their taste warrants.

Coffee, *arabica* or *robusta*, is grown on farms ranging from thousands of acres where the beans are mechanically harvested to one woman tending her quarter acre or even less in a coffee cooperative. The coffee trees are germinated and nurtured in shaded nurseries. When the seedlings are about sixteen inches tall, they are set out. The trees will grow to be eight to thirty feet tall.

Four to five years after planting, the trees bear their first cranberry-shaped red fruit, called cherries. They will continue to produce for fifty to sixty years (and some have endured a century). The average tree will produce about ten pounds of "cherries" a year. Inside the mucilaginous red pulp of the cherry, a parchment coat and silver skin surround the bilobed seed, the coffee bean. After roasting, ten pounds of beans yield about eight pounds of beans ready for grinding and brewing.

In some growing regions, there can be two harvests a year. Handpicked cherries are harvested as they ripen over a couple of weeks. An experienced picker can harvest over one hundred pounds a day. Large farms on flat land can be mechanically harvested, all the cherries at once. Processing involves getting rid of all the cherry except the bean, drying and loading the green coffee beans into jute sacks. The green coffee will end up in a roastery. It can be the world's biggest, the Folgers plant in New Orleans, where multiple roasters turn out hundreds of pounds at a time. Or, it can be a shop owner with a three-pound roaster kept running most of the day.

Green coffee beans. *From Wikimedia Commons. Licensed under the Creative Commons Attribution-Share Alike 2.0 Germany license.*

Roasting green coffee beans unlocks the different aromas and flavors of that coffee. The application of heat, how much heat, how quickly

A Rich History

Coffee cherries. After processing on the farm, ten pounds of cherries will yield two pounds of green coffee beans. *From Wikimedia Commons. Licensed under the Creative Commons Attribution-Share Alike 2.0 Generic license.*

the temperature rises and how long the heat is applied are the variables that make for infinite flavor and aroma profiles. As the temperature of the beans rises, the beans brown. The amino acids break down and combine with the residual sugar to make new molecules. This is called the Maillard reaction after the Frenchman who first explained it a hundred years ago. "The important thing about the Maillard reaction is not the color, it's the flavors and aromas. Indeed, it should be called 'the flavor reaction,' not the 'browning reaction,'" in Nathan Myhrvold's opinion. He continued, "The molecules it produces provide the potent aromas responsible for the characteristic smells of roasting, baking, and frying." The Maillard is a reaction that keeps on giving. "What begins as a simple reaction between amino acids and sugars quickly becomes very complicated: the molecules produced keep reacting in ever more complex ways that generate literally hundreds of various molecules."

Roasting is as much art as science. After roasting, you taste the brewed coffee. It's called cupping. Do you like the aroma, flavor and mouthfeel? If you want a second opinion, you can send off a sample to a professional grader who will cup the coffee and evaluate it. Coffee that scores 80 or above on a standardized scale is considered "specialty coffee."

The National Coffee Association organizes roasts into four categories. Light roasts are roasted to a light brown and are for brewing milder coffees. Medium roasts are brown, with more flavor. This is also known as the American roast, favored in the United States. Medium dark roasts are dark brown, oily and beginning to have a hint of bitterness. Dark roast beans are shiny black, oily and bitter. Dark roast is the New Orleans roast. Espresso, Italian, Viennese and other European coffees also are dark roasted.

The grind affects the flavor and the aroma of the brew. Too coarse a grind, and the water will go through too quickly to extract the aromas and flavors. Too fine, and the coffee can become over-extracted, lacking flavor and taste bitter. The method of brewing determines the grind. Espresso uses a fine grind as the hot water is introduced under pressure by the espresso

Cuppers, the industry term for coffee tasters, score the coffee grounds according to the quality of the aroma. All three cuppers must agree on the score out of 100. If they disagree, the chief cupper is brought in to referee. *From Wikimedia Commons. Licensed under the Creative Commons Attribution-Share Alike 2.0 Generic license.*

machine. Coarse grind works for a percolator or French press coffeemaker, to mention only two of at least seven different grinds.

By coffee's "Rule of 15," green coffee beans should be roasted within fifteen months, ground within fifteen days of roasting and brewed and served within fifteen minutes of grinding—in a perfect world.

There is no winter freeze in the tropics, no dormant period when plants gather strength and have a respite from the insects and blights that prey on them. Botanists believe plants evolved to produce chemicals to deter insects and pests. Bitter caffeine is one of them but not the only one. Coffee's caffeine has a lot of company: tea's theophylline and cacao's theobromine. They are alkaloids, organic compounds that have physiological effects on humans. Coffee's caffeine can cause a short, but dramatic, increase in blood pressure and blood vessel constriction and creates a state of mental alertness and readiness. Tea leaves contain caffeine and theophylline. Theophylline is used to treat respiratory diseases such as chronic obstructive pulmonary disease (COPD) and asthma. The cacao seeds used to make cocoa contain theobromine.

Antique Philadelphia Star Mill grinder. *Photo by Suzanne Stone, reprinted with permission of the Southern Food and Beverage Museum.*

Theobromine is a vasodilator (a blood vessel widener), a diuretic (urination aid) and heart stimulant. It's been used to treat high blood pressure. Kola nut extract, used to make cola-flavored "soft drinks," contains about 2 percent caffeine.

Most food historians agree that the custom of eating something sweet with coffee came soon after the drink's introduction into Europe, most likely in Germany. Stuart Berg Flexner claimed that the term "coffee cake" became common in America in 1879.

Breakfast Sausage Spice Cake

2 cups boiling water
1 cup raisins
1 pound bulk pork sausage
1 ½ cups dark brown sugar
1 ½ cups white sugar
2 large eggs, slightly beaten
3 cups all-purpose flour, sifted
1 teaspoon ground ginger
1 teaspoon baking powder
¼ teaspoon allspice
¼ teaspoon freshly grated nutmeg
¼ teaspoon ground mace
1 teaspoon baking soda
1 cup strong cold coffee
1 cup chopped pecans

Preheat oven to 350 degrees. Grease and flour a Bundt pan well. Add boiling water and raisins to a small bowl. Let stand 5 minutes. Drain raisins well and dry on paper towels or a clean cloth.

Meanwhile, in a large mixing bowl, combine sausage, brown sugar and white sugar. Stir until mixture is well blended. Add eggs and beat well. On waxed paper or a paper plate, sift together flour, ginger, baking powder, allspice, nutmeg and mace. In a small bowl, stir baking soda into coffee. Add flour mixture and coffee mixture alternately into meat mixture, beating well after each addition. Add soaked raisins and pecans to batter. Pour into prepared pan. Bake until top is light brown and springs back when touched, about 1 ½ hours.

Cool 15 minutes before removing from pan. Serve slightly warm.

—recipe reprinted with permission from Nancy Tregre Wilson's *Mémère's Country Creole Cookbook*

3

CREOLE COFFEE

Like the Benediction that Follows after Prayer

Visitors to New Orleans today stroll through beautiful Jackson Square to a paved walkway fronting the magnificent Cathedral of St. Louis. On Good Friday in 1788, a fire started in the home of the colony's military treasurer, Vincente Jose Nuñez, just one block from the square, then the treeless brown parade ground for the Spanish military forces. Among the 856 buildings destroyed in the five-hour conflagration was the original modest church that stood on that spot. Today's cathedral was paid for by wealthy Don Andres Almonester y Roxas; construction began in 1789 and was completed in December 1794, the year the church was designated a cathedral.

At that time, New Orleanians were greeted as they exited the cathedral on Sundays by a wide variety of street vendors, known as *vendeuses*, almost all enslaved women working to buy their freedom. Perhaps most appreciated

Church of St. Louis, 1794 (before designation as a cathedral). *From Wikimedia Commons.*

Jackson Square, 2018. *Photo by Suzanne Stone.*

after a morning in church was coffee. Catharine Cole, in her 1916 book, *The Story of the Old French Market New Orleans*, told the tale of "Old Rose," who was allowed to work for herself on Sundays and seized the opportunity she saw: to provide fresh, hot coffee to churchgoers and others congregating in town on Sunday, as well as French Market vendors, workers and shoppers. Old Rose's entrepreneurial efforts were a quick success. As reported in the *Times Picayune*, one customer commented, "Her coffee is like the benediction that follows after prayer." According to Catherine Cole, Old Rose, having bought her freedom, "kept the most famous coffee stall of the old French Market." And here, the coffee may have been more welcome than outside the cathedral. Back then, the streets were, according to Christina Vella, "so incredibly foul that sometimes even carriages could not get through them. They were choked with garbage, filthy as sewers, and always wet."

The French Market was quite a bit different than what people see today. Families, servants and enslaved people joined indigenous people. The buildings were only for butchers and vegetable sellers; everyone else gathered in stalls or under canopies. Todd and April Fell described a place where French, Spanish, German and patois joined the "sounds of caged parrots and monkeys for sale, chickens and turkeys, and perhaps a brass band or an organ grinder in the background." Smells also mingled: molasses, spices, fruits, baked goods, oysters and peppers all overlapping with the aroma of steaming coffee.

A Rich History

Rose Glá, who sold coffee in the lower end of the market, as pictured in the February 1896 issue of *Men and Matters. Photo by Suzanne Stone.*

Old Rose was operating during the Spanish reign, when the locals, whether French or Spanish, drank coffee in abundance. Elizabeth Williams asserted that "New Orleanians drank coffee all day." And this was despite the fact that—in those days—coffee was an imported luxury, among the items that drove Spanish governor Esteban Rodríguez Miró (1782–91) into debt. It is said that he served coffee "in spectacular quantities." That may not be surprising given that, as much as in New Orleans today, coffee is a way of life in Spain. The Spanish may have introduced alcohol in coffee to New Orleans, which was governed by Havana. It is there that Spanish troops added brandy to their coffee for extra courage (*coraje*). Today, the carajillo combines coffee with brandy, whiskey, anisette or rum.

Zabette and Rose Glá* also sold coffee, with Zabette known for a stand directly in front of the cathedral. Rose Glá was described by the *Daily Picayune* "smiling always and amicable as dawn." This could have been part of an unofficial obituary, as the article continued, "Her coffee was the essence of

---

* While some, like the authors of the *Men and Matters* article, see the "Glá" as a possible surname for Rose, others read "Glá" as "Cila," which linguist Alcée Fortier says is a demonstrative adjective, such as "this" or "that" in English, in what he called the "Negro-French" dialect.

the fragrant bean, and since her death the lovers of that divine beverage wander listlessly around the stalls on Sunday mornings with a pining in the bosom that cannot be satisfied."

These women, and other street vendors, may have provided some of their earnings from each Sunday's sales to their owners, as this was the typical arrangement. They saved the portion they were allowed to keep until they had enough to buy their freedom. These arrangements stem from the earliest days of the Louisiana territory. Lacking sufficient laborers among the first population, which included prostitutes and released prisoners—disturbers of the peace, night prowlers and a man who had threatened to kill his mother, according to city records—the French colony of Louisiana brought over 172 people from Africa in two ships in 1719 and enslaved them. These comprised one-third of the population at that time. Over the next twenty-four years, an additional twenty-one ships came to New Orleans, bringing a total of 5,951 Africans. By the end of the French period, in 1762, a majority of people in Louisiana were individuals of African descent born in the colony.

In 1724, the French instituted a Code Noir, based on the Black Code first established in 1685 in French Caribbean colonies. While providing more rights to enslaved people than British and Dutch laws (for example, owners of enslaved people were required to baptize the enslaved in the Catholic faith and to give them Sundays off, and enslaved people were allowed to marry), this code diverged in negative ways from other laws governing enslaved people in many Caribbean colonies. In the French code, masters did not have sole discretion to grant freedom; the Superior Council reviewed and granted (or did not) all requests for freedom. Further, the council required a reason for granting freedom beyond mere generosity.

The second Spanish governor of Louisiana, General Alejandro O'Reilly (1769–70), imposed Spanish law regarding enslaved people in place of French laws. By doing so, he allowed owners to free enslaved people without official permission. In addition, enslaved people had the right to demand contracts to purchase their freedom for an amount determined by an independent assessment; owners could not refuse to free the enslaved person. Ned Sublette stated that 1,330 enslaved people freed themselves under these laws, and another 160 enslaved people were freed by free people of color (as they were then called). These 1,490 were roughly 20 percent of the city's population in 1803.

Women like Zabette, various Roses and the many sellers of other foods whose names were not recorded are important links in the chain of African-inspired food and drink production in New Orleans, a tradition that continues today. Tales of New Orleans through the middle of the twentieth century recall neighborhood vendors. African American women continued the entrepreneurship of their ancestors, selling pralines and *calas*, an African rice fritter or pastry. Women selling calas generally carried them in covered baskets or bowls. And they sang out, "Belle Cala, Tout Chaud" ("Nice Calas, Very Hot"). But one enterprising soul followed Zabette Glá's example or was Zabette's inspiration. She cooked them in a pan on a small furnace she stationed directly in front of the St. Louis Cathedral.

While calas are no longer made commercially, pralines are. The original New Orleans pralines are a candy made from brown sugar and pecans, since the white sugar and almonds needed for the French praline were not available in the colony. Later on, cream and butter and flavorings were added. Food historians say that by the middle of the nineteenth century, many of the praline vendors around town were known by nicknames, such as *Tante* (Aunt) Marie, who sold her goods on Royal Street; Zabet and Praline Zizi, who worked in Jackson Square; and Tante Titine at St. Louis Cathedral. Outside the French Quarter, Mary Louise, known as "praline mammy," vended at Tulane University and Newcomb College, located in uptown New Orleans. Her daughter, Azelie, sold her pralines at the St. Charles Hotel, introducing the historic New Orleans sweet to visitors to the city. While various flavors of pralines have existed since at least Mary Louise's time, according to Chanda Nunez, today pralines and coffee are being blended. Community Coffee offers one blend of coffee flavored with pecan pralines.

Today, the legend of Rose Nicaud embodies for New Orleanians all the stories of Old Rose and Rose Glá. The 1896 drawing of Rose Glá is often used as a drawing of Rose Nicaud. They were the first to bring coffee to the people outside their home. They inspired free women of color in the nineteenth century to start their own stands, serving their own coffee blends. This was the beginning of the New Orleans coffee stand, in a city still home to many independently owned coffee shops. It also was the beginning of a tradition, enjoyed into present time, of attending Sunday mass at St. Louis Cathedral and heading over, afterward, to the French Market for coffee. And it was the beginning of African-born or African-descended women becoming master Creole chefs.

Nancy Tregore Wilson has published her great-grandmother's original and her daughter's more modern recipes for pralines:

Memere's Pralines

Butter
Aluminum foil
1 ¼ cups evaporated milk
1 cup granulated sugar
4 tablespoons dark corn syrup
3 cups pecan halves or pieces
1 ½ teaspoons vanilla extract

Butter 2 feet of aluminum foil. Combine milk, sugar and corn syrup in a heavy-bottomed 3-quart pot. Cook on low heat stirring constantly, until mixture reaches 228 degrees Fahrenheit. Stir in pecans and vanilla and cook to 236 degrees. Remove from heat and stir three minutes. Scoop and drop by tablespoonful onto prepared foil. Cool completely. Store in an airtight container.

• • •

Angela's Microwave Pralines

Butter
Aluminum foil
1 1-pound box of dark-brown sugar
1 cup evaporated milk
¼ cup (½ stick) butter
3 cups shelled pecans
1 tablespoon vanilla extract

Butter 2 feet of aluminum foil. Stir together sugar and evaporated milk in a microwave-safe bowl. Cook in a 1,250-watt microwave oven for 7 minutes on high. Stir in butter. Add pecans and vanilla. Continue stirring until mixture begins to thicken, 3 to 5 minutes. Drop by spoonfuls onto prepared foil. Let set approximately 30 minutes. Store in an airtight container.

A Rich History

Calas

Recipes for homemade calas all call for eggs, sugar and flour to be added to cooked rice and spices, including vanilla, nutmeg and cinnamon. The dough is fried and then served hot, with powdered sugar.

Queens of Creole Cooking

New Orleans boasts three famous Creole cooks, each of whom has included coffee with her many meals. Creole cuisine is, according to New Orleans food historian Ryan Fertel, the cooking of New Orleans and surrounding southeastern Louisiana. It can involve influences from France, Germany, Spain or any of the other nationalities that comprise New Orleans. The first celebrated Creole cook was Elizabeth Kettenring, who emigrated from Germany in 1853. Ten years later, she and her first husband, Louis Dutrey (also known as Dutreuil), opened Dutrey's Coffee House at Decatur and Madison, near the open-air market in the French Quarter. After being widowed, Kettenring married bartender Hypolyte Bégué and, in 1880, changed the name of the coffeehouse to Bégué's. At some point, the establishment began serving a multicourse meal consisting of both breakfast and lunch items for the butchers and others working in the French Market. These folks had been hard at work since dawn, and by closing at 11:00 a.m.–noon, were hot, tired, hungry and thirsty. Their meal at Bégué's could last for hours, as it included six courses and chicory coffee, ending with, as Poppy Tooker describes, "café noir, into which [Mr. Bégué] pours brandy and then burns it." One of the best-known dishes was liver à la Bégué, while her beef brisket with horseradish remains a mainstay today of the successor restaurant, Tujague's.

During the 1884 Cotton Exposition, Bégué's became a top tourist attraction. Guests to the city warmed to the "second breakfast," as Madame Bégué called it, and her wonderful cooking. From this came the publication in 1900 by the Southern Pacific Railroad of *Madame Bégué and Her Recipes: Old Creole Cookery*. The widow of William Sidney Porter, better known as O. Henry, visited Bégué's restaurant after her husband's death. The second Mme. Bégué remembered that O. Henry loved

Creole coffee: "When I see him, I always reach for the coffee biggin." After she tasted the coffee there, Mrs. Porter reminisced that she tried to make New Orleans coffee since her husband loved it so, "but now that I've been here and tasted it, I know the kind I made was a very poor imitation. Why, I always let my coffee boil."

By 1894, Nellie Murray—formerly enslaved and owned by the family of the fourteenth governor of Louisiana, Paul Octave Hébert—was known as the "Queen of New Orleans Creole cuisine," according to the *Daily Picayune*, which stated, "All fashionable New Orleans knows how Nellie is always in demand for every elegant dejeuner a la fourchette, luncheon and swell dinner, and they know that when a 'function' of this kind is placed in her hands their guests will be served with such savory dishes as would make an epicure of Ancient Rome crown her with laurels." She first may have become known outside of Louisiana in 1893, when she was offered an honorable position as chef de cuisine at the Louisiana Mansion Club at the 1893 World's Fair in Chicago. There she became an instant celebrity. Northerners tasting Louisiana Creole cuisine for the first time waited for hours to meet her and relish her elegant menu.

Madame Bégué, the first Queen of Creole Cooking. Photo by Suzanne Stone. Reprinted with permission from Tujague's Restaurant.

Murray used her status for political purposes. Before her death in 1918, she had catered a private luncheon for Susan B. Anthony, spoken out against New Orleans' segregated streetcar laws and made 1,030 sandwiches with her famed drip coffee for American soldiers on their way to Cuba during the Spanish-American War. Many believe she was the bridge between enslaved cooks who were the backbone of the traditional daily feasts and the vendeuses and tantes, all of whom were descendants

Nellie Murray, the second Queen of Creole Cooking. Drawing reproduced with permission from nola.com, the online *Times-Picayune*.

of women brought here from West and Central Africa, with advanced culinary skills, and later well-known Creole cooks, including Leah Chase, chef and owner of the legendary Dooky Chase restaurant.

Leah Chase, the current Queen of Creole Cuisine, began her love affair with food when she worked as a waitress at the old Colonial Hotel. Later she met, fell in love with and married Dooky Chase II. She soon joined the kitchen in his family's street corner stand in Tremé. Over time, she converted the stand into a restaurant and updated the menu to reflect her family's Creole recipes. During the 1960s, Dooky's became known as a gathering place for civil rights activists, including A.P. Tureaud, Ernest "Dutch" Morial and Martin Luther King Jr. Local law enforcement did not stop such meetings, which were illegal at the time, as blacks and whites could not legally congregate in New Orleans. Chase's philosophy that good food brings people together inspired the directors of Disney's *Princess and the Frog* in their depiction of her as Princess Tiana.

Photographic portrait of Leah Chase taken at Dooky Chase from Blake Nelson Boyd's "Louisiana Cereal." *From Wikimedia Commons.*

Chase has advocated passionately for African American art and for Creole cooking. In 2013, she and her husband founded the Edgar "Dooky" Jr. and Leah Chase Family Foundation to "cultivate and support historically disenfranchised organizations by making significant contributions to education, creative and culinary arts, and social justice."

4

THE DAWN OF AMERICAN NEW ORLEANS

Antebellum Markets

As the nineteenth century dawned, change and explosive growth defined New Orleans life. In a few decades, the city went from a small port to a thriving, bustling metropolis. The revolution in Saint-Domingue was instrumental in this. Saint-Domingue was one of France's most financially successful colonies. Enslaved people lived and worked under particularly brutal conditions on the coffee and sugar cane plantations. Yellow fever killed about 50 percent of the Africans, which justified to their owners the situation of working the people as hard as possible while providing them with the minimum of food and other necessities. They wanted to obtain the most work possible before the enslaved people died. Such conditions gave rise to the successful revolution, leading to the establishment of Haiti. Napoleon was disinclined to give up Haiti and tried to retake it. This was not to be: Napoleon lost tens of thousands of his army of fifty-four thousand, including his brother-in-law General LeClerc, to battle and disease trying to retake the former colony. On Easter Sunday, 1803, Napoleon resolved to sell all of Louisiana.

President Jefferson's negotiators had arrived shortly before that Easter day and offered to buy New Orleans. To their surprise, Napoleon countered by offering all of Louisiana at a higher price. A deal was struck for $15 million. The United States did not have that much money, so the government borrowed the money from the British and gave it to Napoleon, who used it to finance his coming battles, including those with the British. On December 20, 1803, the French flag came down and the

American flag went up, effecting the transfer of Louisiana from France to the United States.

During 1809 and 1810, about nine thousand Saint-Domingue refugees arrived in Louisiana. This bump in population doubled the size of New Orleans and resulted in a population that was roughly one-third white, one-third free people of color and one-third enslaved people. The free Saint-Domingue refugees, both white and of color, were well educated and, quite often, wealthy. They had a disproportionately large influence on New Orleans life, especially in the French Quarter and other Creole neighborhoods, in the first half of the nineteenth century. They increased the Creole influence. They brought with them the shotgun architecture style, still prevalent throughout the city. Also, since Saint-Domingue had been supplying 50 percent of the world's coffee, many were involved in the coffee trade and brought that expertise to New Orleans.

One of the major auctioneers in New Orleans was Joseph LeCarpentier, a Saint-Domingue refugee. In the 1820s, he built the well-known Beauregard-Keyes House (named for General Pierre Gustave Toutant-Beauregard, who lived there after the Civil War, and novelist Frances Parkinson Keyes, the last owner and resident).

Even before the Saint-Domingue refugees arrived, people from the U.S. frontier began to move in. What those first Anglo-Protestant Americans found was a Catholic, multicultural, multiracial and multilingual city unlike anywhere else in the United States. They also found a city passionate about its uniquely flavored coffee. Later, people with capital from the border states and northeastern United States arrived, and these men would make and lose fortunes in trade and trade-related industries, including coffee.

As New Orleans and the rest of the Louisiana Territory became American, coffeehouses and coffee exchanges of many types sprang up. Nothing of the sort existed in 1806, when a traveler—Thomas Ashe—noted that "there is no exchange nor any other general place of mercantile resort." Later in the year, others noted that the city now had two banks and one exchange, soon known as *the* Exchange, on the upper side of Conti Street, between Decatur and Chartres. As noted architect and historian Samuel Wilson Jr., stated, this was when the "practice of combining business functions with those of a coffeehouse began and continued for many years."

In this, New Orleans was following the rich tradition of the Ottoman "schools of wisdom," France's Café Procope and England's "penny universities." Throughout coffee's history, establishments set up to serve coffee facilitated ancillary functions. They brought people together to share knowledge and provided a place for private and public conversations. They later became meeting places for revolutionaries. Politics also came to the fore when colonists in the United States turned to coffee instead of tea, a blatantly political act. Coffeehouses were ideal places for those who were politically motivated to meet. Daniel Webster stated that the famous Green Dragon Coffee House in Boston was "headquarters of the Revolution." George Washington, Thomas Jefferson, Benjamin Franklin, Gilbert du Motier, the Marquis de Lafayette and John Adams were all known to frequent the Merchant's Coffee House in Philadelphia.

New Orleans also was following the tradition of conducting business in coffeehouses, such as the Tontine Coffee House in New York, which became the home of the New York Stock Exchange. Earlier, London's Lloyd's Coffee House, where sailors, merchants and shipowners drank coffee and discussed shipping news, became an ideal place for obtaining marine insurance, including insurance on slave ships and enslaved people. Over time, this grew into Lloyd's of London, an insurance market.

Coffeehouses and coffee exchanges in New Orleans served all these purposes. They were places to drink coffee, the most popular nonalcoholic beverage in town; read any of the numerous daily newspapers; gather with men of similar minds about politics; discuss the most current artistic or intellectual news; and carry on trade. As a sign of the amount of discourse and business in New Orleans, the second coffeehouse and exchange was opened in 1811, at the corner of Chartres and St. Louis Streets. This was to be—for the next decades—the best-known coffee exchange in the city. It was leased to Bernard Tremoulet and first called the Commercial Exchange, then the New Exchange and popularly known as Tremoulet's Exchange. Soon thereafter, the lease of the coffeehouse passed to Pierre Maspero, who was already leasing the building next to it and operating it as a mirror and framing shop. After Maspero's death in 1822, the establishment was known as Elkins Coffee House; in 1832, it was taken over by James Hewlett and known as Hewlett's Exchange.

As New Orleans continued to prosper and grow into the 1830s, American businesses organized the Merchant's Exchange, on Royal Street, near Canal. Soon thereafter, the St. Charles Exchange Hotel opened in the American sector of the city. Creole businessmen countered with the St. Louis Hotel, running the full block from Royal to Chartres Streets, on St. Louis. One of them was Samuel Jarvis Peters, a Canadian who apprenticed in a French counting house in New York. In New Orleans, he married a Creole from a prominent family and went into the wholesale grocery business and politics.

The foundation stone for the St. Louis Hotel was laid in 1836. The hotel was considered one of the most striking structures of the city until destroyed by a hurricane in 1915. *From Wikimedia Commons.*

He was one of the few at that time to successfully bridge the cultural divide between the Creoles and Anglos.

Another of the city's oldest coffeehouses was Gwathmey's Coffee House, at the southwest corner of Conti and Chartres Streets. "In the early days of the American domination, it was a popular rendezvous and here, at old 45 Chartres Street. John Gwathmey had his celebrated coffee-house and John James Audubon visited him here," said Stanley Clisby Arthur. This celebrated coffeehouse later became the Merchants' Coffee House and eventually the Phoenix Oyster and Beefsteak House. The lot it was built on belonged to the widow of Vincent Rillieux, and when the property was sold in 1842 by the Rillieux Carmouche family, "the new owner had to agree to care for the vendor, Mlle. Marie Calliste Carmouche, a maiden lady of advanced years, for the rest of her life!" The Rillieux family was one that immigrated from Saint-Domingue. Vincent Rillieux first appears in New Orleans history during the American Revolutionary War. Spain offered support to the colonists with trade from, among other places, New Orleans and in battles against the British. One battle occurred on the Amite River, where two English troop ships were captured, with credit being given to New Orleanian Vincent Rillieux.

Self-portrait of Edgar Degas. Vincent Rillieux's niece Marie Celestine Musson was the mother of impressionist painter Edgar Degas. Vincent also was the father of free man of color Norbert Rillieux, inventor of the renowned "triple evaporation pan system," for processing and refining sugar. *From Wikimedia Commons. Licensed under the Creative Commons Attribution-Share Alike 4.0 International license.*

There were literally dozens of coffeehouses in the French Quarter, so many that the names of some are lost to history. A less-well-known coffeehouse started in 1816, at the corner of Chartres and Wilkinson Streets, as soon as that street—named for now-disgraced American soldier James Wilkinson—was cut through. Next door was Monsieur Charles, a "coiffeur." Stanley Clisby Arthur maintains that women would get their hair styled in the latest Parisian fashion "while their husbands and sons [went to] the corner café." By 1850, there were over five hundred coffeehouses and coffee exchanges in the city, including the Empire, the Gem and the Ruby. The Gem, at 127–29 Royal Street, which now houses the Unique Grocery, started as a home for a Spanish nobleman and was the birthplace of the Mistick Krewe of Comus.

Politics

Tremoulet's was the site, said Charles Cassady Jr., of competing postings of bounties. First, Governor William C.C. Claiborne posted a bounty of $500 for Jean Laffite, noted privateer, pirate and later defender of the city with General Andrew Jackson at the Battle of New Orleans. Next, Lafitte posted his handbill offering a reward of $1,000 for anyone who could capture Governor Claiborne and deliver him to Lafitte.

Tremoulet's also is where the convention met that resulted in Louisiana's being admitted to the United States as the eighteenth state in 1812. In 1814, the "Committee of Public Defence" met at Tremoulet's to call for unity among the French and American populations in the upcoming battle against the British. The committee's gatherings at the Exchange, now known as Maspero's, recounted Stanley Clisby Arthur, "welded the citizens of the city into one fighting unit when General Andrew Jackson arrived." And Maspero's is where "an indignant crowd of citizens" brought General Jackson after he had been held in contempt of court.

A notice in the August 8, 1826 *Louisiana State Gazette* stated:

> *We have learnt with concern, that the City Council could come to no conclusion yesterday, as to a mode of testifying the regret which Louisiana feels at the loss which the nation has sustained in the death of* THOMAS JEFFERSON *and* JOHN ADAMS, *two of the most distinguished civil chiefs of the revolution.... Call for people to meet at Hewlett's Coffee House this*

> *evening at seven o'clock, to consult on such measures as may be expedient to express the high sense which the people of Louisiana entertain of the eminent services rendered to this republic by Thomas Jefferson and John Adams.*

Clearly, a meeting at one of the city's oldest and best-known coffeehouses would resolve matters that the city council was unable to decide.

Important institutions were established and officers elected in coffeehouses. In February 1808, the officers of the city's chamber of commerce were elected at the Exchange. The April 29, 1850 issue of the *Daily Picayune* reported, "Citizens in the fifth ward organized themselves as Fire Company 21. The election took place at the Globe Coffee House." Similarly, on page 4 of the *Daily Picayune* of December 26, 1852, it was announced that meetings of "Inspectors and Clerks of the Election" of each precinct were to be held. Of the twenty-three precincts, four held meetings held at coffeehouses: "J. Henderson's Coffee House, Orleans Coffee House, D. Altmau's Coffee House," and the "coffeehouse [on the] east corner of Bayou Road and St. Claude Streets."

The Gem played a role in Reconstruction politics. Governor Henry Clay Warmoth (1868–72) was charged with receiving bribes, stealing public funds and being "the greatest living practical liar."* Because of fighting between Warmoth and his opponents, Speaker of the Louisiana House of Representatives G.W. Carter was "compelled to seat the House of Representatives in the hall above the Gem Saloon" on January 5, 1872, according to Ned Hémard. Warmoth proclaimed the Gem "House" as "revolutionary, unconstitutional and illegal." Warmoth was impeached and suspended, paving the way for Lieutenant Governor P.B.S. Pinchback to be sworn in as the first state governor of African descent in the United States.

FOOD AND DRINK

Lunches were often served in coffeehouses. The November 20, 1826 issue of the *Louisiana State Gazette* provided a notice of the menu at the Globe Coffee House: "Oysters, Mutton, Beef Chops to be furnished at all hours of the day and evening. Likewise, breakfast and dinners." Deidre Stanforth's history of

---

* Henry Clay Warmoth replied, "I don't pretend to be honest. I only pretend to be as honest as anybody in politics."

New Orleans restaurants states that the "free lunch" originated in the Old St. Louis Hotel. It offered a free noontime meal as the city expanded and businessmen were not able to get home for noontime dinner, which was the main meal of the day. As can be imagined, the practice was very much appreciated, and the hotel was unable to stop it later. In fact, other "drinking establishments" also introduced the "free lunch," which, in reality, was paid for by the extra drinks ordered by customers staying longer. The custom spread to other establishments.

These "free lunches" changed not just dining habits but dining times for New Orleans. Marguerite Samuels wrote in 1920 in the *Times-Picayune* that the Gem's owner, in the 1840s, posted the manifests of ships' cargoes. Merchants now could bypass the wharf and head to the Gem for business and enjoy a midday dinner, provided free of charge with fifteen cents' worth of whiskey. The story goes that so many businessmen then worked late or otherwise did not return home for the usual supper time, which meant a late evening meal "became a fixture in New Orleans." Returning home was not the same kind of stroll it is today in a small city. In the 1840s, sidewalks were flagged or bricked for only a few blocks, and as Eliza Reilly recalled, "If it was near Christmas time…we might meet a flock of turkeys marching up Camp Street.…In those days fowls were not offered for sale ready dressed or plucked, but sold 'on the hoof,' as we say of cattle."

The Globe's 1826 menu was typical of the substantial fare offered in the beginning, which appears to have continued for some time, as a *New York Times* reporter called the meal "hearty" and described it as containing bread and butter, "a monster silver boiler filled with a most excellent oyster soup," "a round of beef that must have weighed at least forty pounds" and "vessels filled with potatoes, stewed mutton, stewed tomatoes, and macaroni *à la Français*." Most places eventually reduced their meals to cheese, cold cuts and bread. From this, of course, comes today's practice of complimentary snacks at happy hour.

This New Orleans custom gained prominence throughout the country. In 1875, the *New York Times* wrote of free lunches as a "custom peculiar to the Crescent City," saying, "In every one of the drinking saloons which fill the city a meal of some sort is served free every day.…I am informed that there are thousands of men in this city who live entirely on the meals obtained in this way."

Both coffeehouses and coffee exchanges sold alcoholic beverages, sometimes in the evening only. In the late 1840s, Sewell Taylor owned the Merchants Exchange Coffee House and became the sole importer in New

Orleans of a cognac made by Sazerac du Forge et Fils. When importing proved successful, Taylor sold the exchange coffeehouse to Aaron Bird, who renamed the business the Sazerac Coffee House. Antoine Amédée Peychaud, a friend and apothecary, meanwhile had invented an aniseed and gentian bitters at his shop, the Pharmacie Peychaud. This was served in *coquetiers* (little egg cups). Together Bird and Peychaud invented the Sazerac cocktail. Bird rinsed a glass with absinthe before dropping in a sugar cube and adding cognac and Peychaud's bitters. Later, rye whiskey replaced the cognac. Renowned New Orleans philanthropist William Goldring now owns the company started at that coffeehouse. In 1949, the Roosevelt Hotel bought Peychaud's recipe and opened the Sazerac Bar in the hotel.

Sales

The biggest difference between a coffeehouse and a coffee exchange was that, like New York's Tontine Coffee House and London's Lloyd's Coffee House, sales were made at coffee exchanges. Many coffeehouses turned into exchanges. Given that New Orleans became, in the decades from 1830 to 1860, the country's largest slave market, New Orleans coffee exchanges and the slave trade are inextricably tied together. In 1812, the same year Louisiana entered the United States as the eighteenth state, the steamboat was introduced to New Orleans—vastly accelerating trade up the Mississippi River—and the law made importation of Africans a felony. Thus, just as hundreds of thousands of immigrants and Americans were moving south and westward, where the cotton economy was booming, a huge demand for American-born slave labor was developing.

New Orleans was an established trade city, with control over the Mississippi River and access to the Gulf of Mexico. Before the Civil War, close to one million enslaved people were brought by boat, rail, stagecoach and foot to reach New Orleans and be sold. Of the fifty-two slave markets in the city, the largest was in the eighty-eight-foot-tall rotunda of the St. Louis Hotel. Sales of enslaved people were held from noon to 3:00 p.m. daily. Brett Todd, Kate Mason and Kathryn O'Dwyer reported that "numerous 19th-century travelers who frequented New Orleans for business and pleasure described the slave auction block in the St. Louis Hotel. Sensationalism aside, visitors recorded their surprise at the grandeur and spectacle of the Hotel's exchange area, which functioned as a sort of auction theater."

Early twentieth-century photo postcard showing an African American woman standing on half-ruined slave block, in the Old St. Louis Hotel, where she had been sold as a child. *From Wikimedia Commons.*

Many assume that in one or both of his visits to New Orleans, Abraham Lincoln would have seen the sales at the St. Louis. "Innumerable histories and biographies have deduced one core narrative from Lincoln's flatboat journeys: that the sight of slavery in New Orleans…helped convince the young man of the institution's moral bankruptcy."

Samples from advertisements for sales in various coffee exchanges:

> *March 18, 1818,* New Orleans Argus *(published as* L'Ami des Lois et Journal du Soir*), page 4: "Court of Probates—Sale by the Register of Wills. A mulatto named Charlotte, a native of Virginia, about 40 years of age, laundress belonging to the estate of the late Thomas Birot, will be exposed for sale at the French coffee house, on Thursday the 9th of April next, Monday 23rd of March next, at 12 o'clock."*

> *July 25, 1820,* Louisiana Advertiser, *page 2: "Sale at Auction by Joseph Le Carpentier This day, at 1 o'clock, at Maspero's Coffee House, will be sold with no reserve, 2 negro Men, field hands."*

> *January 11, 1843, the* Daily Picayune, *page 3, provides a listing of fifteen people who will be "sold at auction, Friday, the 13th inst., at Banks' Arcade." After the list appears this statement: "The above Negroes are fully guaranteed, excepting Mary, who occasionally drinks."*

A Rich History

Socializing

It was not all business. The April 18, 1819 entry in Benjamin Latrobe's* diary reads, "On coming near the French Coffee House, I heard the blow of the cue and the rebound of billiards balls upstairs. The coffeehouse was full." And William Norris described the interiors of places like the Gem and Ruby as "furnished with thick carpets, easy chairs, gilded mirrors, gas-lit chandeliers, newspapers, and paintings of a reclining nude over the bar mantle [sic]."

As Richard Campanella explained, discussing Abraham Lincoln's travels to New Orleans as a flatboat merchant, "'Exchange,' by the 1820s, implied a full-service business-networking center, where white men could convene, discuss, negotiate, socialize, recreate, gamble, dine, drink, and board.... Like many of New Orleans' 'coffeehouses,' the upper floors [of Hewlett's] contained billiards and gambling tables." Importantly, New Orleanian businessmen conducted business or argued politics leisurely, in a coffeehouse, not an office.

Coffee

The many coffeehouses served important political and business purposes, but first and foremost, they served coffee, as did coffee stands, run by free people of color, in various markets throughout the city. Mary Gehman presented the story of Agnes, who is listed in city directories as having a permanent coffee stand in the Poydras Market in 1853. This market was outside the French Quarter; wherever immigrants to New Orleans moved—to the new neighborhoods of the American sector, the Marigny, the Tremé, uptown and toward the lakes on high ridges—coffeehouses could be found. Mary Lou Widmer recalled a grocery store in her 1930s City Park neighborhood that began as a coffeehouse in 1860. It is now a restaurant, Ralph's on the Park, and the land on which the building stands was part of a tract owned originally by the city's founder, sieur de Bienville. An earlier restaurant—at the turn of the twentieth century—was

---

* Noted architect Benjamin Henry Boneval Latrobe and his son came to New Orleans to plan for a city waterworks system based on their plan for the one they had developed in Philadelphia in response to Philadelphia's yellow fever epidemics. Unfortunately, both father and son died of yellow fever in New Orleans, and their plans never materialized.

A Lá Renaissance des Chenes Verts. According to Mary Lou Widmer, on Sunday afternoons, the ladies from Storyville (New Orleans' sanctioned red light district) "in their daring décolletage, their enormous feathered hats, and their beads and jewels, drove to the Chenes Verts in their fine carriages."

Clearly, the city's nineteenth-century denizens continued the fondness for coffee first exhibited by the French and Spanish. And the many newcomers also enjoyed coffee, whether of the Creole style or their own. The December 13, 1841 *Weekly Picayune* refers to a "German Coffee House." Christina Vella reported, "German was heard in the coffeehouses and feed stores as often as French."

However, new uses for coffee also were being discovered. Louise McKinney pointed out that nineteenth-century Creole women "also managed to find an external use for it, darkening their hair with coffee grinds at the first sign of gray."

Coffee Hair Dye

Even today, coffee can be used to darken hair. A search of the internet turns up numerous "recipes" for using dark coffee or espresso and hair conditioner. Also, coffee is becoming part of other foods, such as breakfast cereal.

• • •

Dairy- and Gluten-Free Coffee Granola

3½ cups old-fashioned rolled oats (gluten free, if desired)
¼ cup chopped raw pecans
¼ cup flax meal
¼ cup chopped Medjool dates (pitted)
¼ cup coffee grounds (be sure to use a coffee you really like)
½ cup runny almond butter (I like Trader Joe's Raw Creamy Almond Butter)
½ cup brown rice syrup
1 tablespoon pure vanilla extract
½ teaspoon sea salt
2 tablespoons water (to thin)

Preheat oven to 325 degrees. Combine oats, pecans, flax meal, dates and ground coffee in a large mixing bowl. In a small pot on the stove over medium-low heat, combine the almond butter, brown rice syrup, vanilla extract, salt and water. Whisk until smooth. If the mixture seems too thick, add additional water 1 tablespoon at a time until pourable.

Pour the almond butter mixture over the oats mixture. Stir well to ensure all the dry ingredients are moistened. Spread the mixture in fairly even layer onto a rimmed baking sheet, but with very little, if any, space between the ingredients. This is how you'll get the nice big clumps of granola! Bake for 25–28 minutes, shaking the pan and flipping the mixture over as best you can about halfway through. The granola will continue to crisp up as it sits, so don't overbake or it will burn. Let cool before eating. Store any leftovers in an airtight container on the counter for 3–4 days.

—Permission to reprint by Jenn Sebestyen and Veggie Inspired. Find full recipe and instructions at https://www.veggieinspired.com/coffee-granola.

5

COFFEE AT HOME

Despite the preponderance of coffeehouses in New Orleans by 1850, most people were imbibing at home. After all, the coffeehouses and coffee exchanges were institutions that served many purposes beyond that of drinking coffee. And coffee was sold to consumers as early as the Spanish period. Governor Alejandro O'Reilly regulated the sale of coffee and other drinks in 1769.

Even the city's architecture attests to the love of coffee. A house at 707–9 Dumaine Street, built in 1800, has a flat tile roof, which was required briefly in the city's fire code. There also is a tall tiled parapet, which hid the roof where the "inhabitants relaxed with their brioche and café au lait in the morning," according to Roulhac Toledano.

And many stories tell how important coffee was in nineteenth-century New Orleans. Eliza Ripley, in her memoir of life in the city in the mid-nineteenth century, recounts her first visitor when she was a new wife in 1852: "a distinguished, eccentric, literary man, a bachelor, and a Creole, brim full of cranks and kinks, but a delightful conversationalist withal….I was amazed when my housemaid told me he had not only brought his valet, but his own linen sheets and coffee pot!"

Ripley also reminisced about a visit to the plantation of François-Gabriel "Valcour" Aimé. When she woke up, "The sun was already proclaiming a bright spring day when I inhaled the odor, and opened my eyes to a full-blown rose on my pillow; and gracious, how good! A steaming cup of café au lait." Riley's host was known as the "Louis XIV of Louisiana."

707–9 Dumaine Street. *Photograph by David Feldman.*

By the 1830s, his St. James Refinery Plantation in Vacherie, Louisiana (about fifty-seven miles upriver from New Orleans), was the leading sugar producer in the world. Aimé prided himself on his plantation's self-sufficiency, and according to Susan Thomas, Aimé wagered $10,000 that he could produce from his plantation alone an entire meal complete with wine, coffee and cigars. After the meal, the guest with whom he'd wagered was shown the plantation hothouses, where both coffee and tobacco were growing. Aimé won the bet.

For proper café au lait, served at breakfast, as Ripley remembered, one first made strong black coffee, then boiled milk and added it to the coffee. Elizabeth M. Williams asserted that it was drunk "in the French manner from large bowls." She also said that "Parisian-style demitasses of dark black coffee were served after evening meals." Although café au lait was the preferred breakfast drink, at other times, coffee was served "black as the devil, strong as death, sweet as love, and hot as hell" (or, in the original

French rhyme, "Noir comme le Diable; Fort comme la Mort; Doux comme l'Amour; Et chaud comme l'Enfer").

Gaspar Stall, a chronicler of New Orleans, said that the coffee, often mixed with chicory, "sometimes got so strong when slow dripped, a spoon of water at a time, that when finished the coffee would get up and get its own sugar." Todd and April Fell said that New Orleanians' drip process was to pour "only a half cup of [boiling] water at first, over the grounds, just to moisten them. Each addition of water was a half cup, and only added when the previous water had dripped through. If it was not strong enough, the coffee would be poured through again, a little at a time." Nancy Tregere Wilson recalled her grandmother's recipe for "Old Fashioned Louisiana Drip Coffee" as using 1½ to 2 tablespoons of drip ground coffee or coffee with chicory and 1 cup of boiling water. She says one poured "¼ cup boiling water at a time over the grounds every few minutes until all water has dripped through the grounds." Then the coffee was heated in a saucepan over low heat. She admonished, "Never boil the coffee."

Lyle Saxon, Edward Dreyer and Robert Tallant recalled a woman of the 1800s remembering her nurse, known as "Mammy," who was interred in the family tomb in St. Louis Cemetery No. 2: "The greatest treat of all was to awaken every morning to Mammy's words, 'Alà vous café,' and see her standing beside your bed…a tray in her hands on which was piping-hot drip coffee, ground and roasted at home."

German New Orleanians had their own coffee customs; John Nau spoke of Sunday afternoons when friends and neighbors would gather to break up "the humdrum and monotony of everyday life." The men would play cards and drink beer, and the women would indulge in a kaffeeklatsch (literally, "coffee gossip") with coffee, and kuchen. In 1933, almost 100 years after German kaffeeklatsch began in New Orleans homes, a local baker, Beulah Levy Ledner, developed a Doberge cake, adapted from the Dobos cake, which originated in Alsace and Lorraine, as did so many of the Germans in New Orleans. Ledner replaced the Dobos cake's buttercream with custard and iced the cakes with buttercream and a thin layer of fondant. While the Doberge cake was not needed to popularize serving coffee at home, it certainly added to the joy of a get-together with friends. Today, the popular dessert can still be purchased in and around New Orleans.

Coffee also played a role in celebrations. Members of German societies celebrated arrivals of German ships. There would be speeches, singing and much eating and drinking. The large meals—which could include turkey, beef and pheasant, cheese and dessert—were punctuated with servings of coffee. Coffee also was featured in family celebrations. Louise McKinney points out that the annual "Christmas Reveillon feasts traditionally concluded with steamy brandy-fortified, orange-laced café brûlot ladled from a Sheffield brûlot bowl." New Orleans' epicurean history credits Antoine Alciatore for inventing this drink at his eponymous restaurant, Antoine's, which opened in 1840. Interestingly, William Ukers wrote, in his discussion of New Orleans coffeehouses, that "the brûleau, coffee with orange juice, orange peel, and sugar, with cognac burned and mixed in it, originated in the New Orleans coffee house, and led to its gradual evolution into the saloon."

Called Café Brûlot Diabolique, it is traditionally prepared tableside with lights dimmed just before flaming. Tish Casey, native New Orleanian, remembers her parents' dinner parties when she was in grade school:

> *Everyone dressed very elegantly and at the end of the evening, I was allowed to join them for the ceremony of making the brûlot. My mom had a copper chafing dish. There were cinnamon sticks, sugar cubes, and orange peels in there. Brandy was added. My father would lift the brandy-soaked orange peel and light it. It would flame up and set the brandy in the chafing dish alight, which was an amazing sight to a kid like me. She would add coffee and use an ornate ladle to transfer it to coffee cups!*

As described by Nora McGunnigle:

> *The drink involves skills like cutting one long piece of peel off an orange, and juggling that task with integrating the coffee to the brandy that's already aflame while handling specialized equipment. There's the silver bowl that holds the brandy and coffee, which is placed on top of a tray filled with more brandy. The booze on the tray is set on fire, heating the brandy and coffee mixture in the silver bowl above it. Then, a ladleful of the potion in the bowl is used to bring the flame into the vessel, so that's on fire now, too. While the mixture is flaming, the server holds the long orange peel over it and ladles flaming cups of coffee and brandy over the peel, which creates a ribbon of blue and orange light traveling down the citrus rind. Usually, the establishment's lights are dimmed to enhance the effect, creating an impressive sight that's quintessential New Orleans in its mix of drink and flamboyance, as if someone once thought, "You know what would make this after-dinner coffee better? Booze and fire."*

A Rich History

Engraving drawn by John Durkin showing New Orleanians decorating the tombs on All Saints' Day. *From Wikimedia Commons.*

According to Elizabeth Williams, "This flavor was duplicated in a soda that was available for a short time in the early twentieth century. The soda, called Café Nola (brulo) was made by the Grunwald Catering Company. The red-suited devil was used in advertising the drink."

In her cultural history, McKinney also described the observance of All Saints' Day, where those New Orleanian gustatory staples—coffee and gumbo—"were even sold in the cemeteries as families cleaned and whitewashed the monuments of their ancestors."

The importance of coffee also is obvious from the care with which it was prepared after the green coffee beans were purchased at the local grocery store. New Orleanians—and their neighbors throughout Southern Louisiana—did not boil the ground coffee in water, since boiling water destroys the delicate, volatile core of the coffee flavor. The French were in the forefront of developing methods of brewing coffee to enhance the flavor and reduce the grounds in the finished product. In France in 1711, just before New Orleans was founded, people had begun infusion brewing: placing the roasted, ground coffee beans in a linen bag and letting them steep, much as tea does, in hot water.

The first drip coffee pot was invented in about 1800 by Jean Baptiste de Belloy, Archbishop of Paris. Ground coffee could be placed in an upper portion of a two-chamber pot, with a cloth lining the opening between the two pots. Hot—not boiling—water was poured over the grounds, and coffee would drip through to the bottom chamber. Unfortunately, the process was so slow that the coffee was lukewarm. The next innovation was the *biggin*, developed in France in the late eighteenth century. This is a two-level pot with a long spout. The coffee is placed on a cloth container

New Orleans Coffee

Coffee biggin. *Photographed by Suzanne Stone, with permission to use from New Orleans' Lucullus Culinary Arts and Objects.*

in the upper chamber. Water is poured into that chamber and drains through holes in the bottom into the coffee pot below, which was used to serve. It has been suggested that the name came from the Dutch word *beggelin*, to "trickle, or run down," although Morton Satin claims a Monsieur Biggin invented the pot. A major problem with this approach was that the taste of the cloth filter—whether cotton, burlap or an old sock—transferred to the taste of the coffee.

By the nineteenth century, in New Orleans, every home had a coffee roaster, a coffee grinder and equipment with which to make coffee from the grounds, usually a biggin. Some may have moved on to the more modern French press, invented about 1850 in France.

Germans may have used vacuum coffee pots, first invented in Berlin in the 1830s. These work by heating water in a lower chamber until, because the water has expanded with the heat, hot water is forced through a narrow tube into an upper chamber that holds ground coffee. When all the water is in the upper chamber and the coffee has finished brewing, the heat is removed, and the resulting vacuum pulls the coffee back through a strainer into the lower chamber, from which it is served.

Roasting could be done in earthenware dishes or saucepans. Mortars and box mills were commonly used for grinding. The quality of the brewed coffee depended, in large part, on the roasting and the grinding. If the grounds were too coarse, the coffee would be weak. If the grounds were too fine, the water would not drip through at the proper speed. This same conundrum has challenged manufacturers of modern coffee grinders. As early as 1840, New Orleanians could forego home roasting and grinding and buy ground coffee beans at William Cochrane's at the corner of Canal and Tremé Streets.

The biggin, or *une greque*, was improved upon by Benjamin Thompson, who, in the late 1700s, enclosed the drip coffee pot in an insulating jacket to keep the coffee hot. The next improvement in coffee making was a pumping percolator, also developed in France. In these devices, water is placed in the bottom compartment and ground coffee above. Then the pot is put on a fire

A Rich History

Right: Coffee grinder.
Photographed by Suzanne Stone with permission to use from New Orleans' Lucullus Culinary Arts and Objects.

Below: Coffee roaster.
Photographed by Suzanne Stone with permission to use from New Orleans' Lucullus Culinary Arts and Objects.

or burner; when the water boils, it is forced up through a tube to the upper chamber and then trickles or percolates through the ground coffee back into the bottom chamber.

The 1901 *Picayune's Creole Cookbook* devotes an entire chapter to Creole Coffee. It was said that "the Creoles hold as a physiological fact that this custom [of drinking *café noir*] contributes to longevity." Residents then also claimed that the cup of coffee after dinner helped with digestion, and coffee was credited as "one of the best preventives for infectious diseases," "an antidote for poison" and "the greatest brain food." In its instructions section, the book claimed one must start with a mix of mocha and java. It is essential to "parch" the coffee right before grinding and brewing. From there on, the instructions emphasize the slow dripping of the coffee. This book also imparts a tip: dropping a bit of charcoal into a cup of coffee that is a muddy or not clear will clear it out.

Later in the twentieth century, Leah Chase recalled that breakfast was coffee and bread, most commonly a biscuit with homemade strawberry jelly. Chase was the exception. She did not know why, but she had cocoa instead of coffee with her condensed milk. Through her adulthood, she did not particularly care for coffee, until she tasted espresso. As she said, "I like things that hang on the tongue." Growing up in rural Louisiana, in part during the Depression, Chase recalled that she and her brothers and sisters went off to school with that breakfast, and she said they "were expected to do well in school, without any need for orange juice, eggs, or some things other people said were necessary later on."

6
CHICORY

Common chicory is a perennial herbaceous plant of the dandelion family, usually with blue flowers and more rarely with white or pink flowers. So much less esteemed than coffee, even chicory's history as a beverage is difficult to trace. Its first use, recorded over 3,000 years ago, was medicinal. Around 1500 BC (some say as early as 5,000 years ago), Egyptians used *Cichorium intybus*—the original name for chicory—to treat intestinal worms and as an aid to digestion. Most likely, the chicory plant's flowers and leaves were used. Within 1,500 years, chicory was commonly used as a liver tonic in Rome; the poet Horace described his diet: "As for me, olives, endives, and mallows provide sustenance." During the Middle Ages, medieval monks cultivated chicory and introduced it to Europe.

It is the chicory plant's roots that are ground and made into powder to blend and mix with coffee. The first written mention of a chicory drink appears to be from Prospero Alpini, an Italian physician and botanist in 1592. One hundred years later, the Dutch roasted the chicory root and both added it to coffee and used it as a coffee substitute. By the mid-1760s, chicory plantations existed in France and Prussia. Not surprisingly then, in 1766, when Frederick the Great of Prussia imposed heavy taxes on coffee and imposed strict licensing regulations on coffee roasting, which made coffee out of reach for most people, chicory came into use as a coffee substitute there. Many reasons have been given for Frederick's act. Some believe he thought coffee a luxury that the masses did not deserve, even though they did not brew it as he did, with champagne instead of water. In the edict, he blamed "the amount of money going out of the country" and mandated, "My people must drink beer," because he had grown up drinking beer. But his people had already developed a taste for coffee, as we can see in Bach's 1732 "Coffee Cantata," where a young woman sings

No lover shall woo me
Unless I have his pledge
Written in the marriage settlement
That he will allow me
To drink coffee when I please

Of many substitutes that were tried for the much-loved coffee, chicory came out on top. Chicory's coffee-like flavor comes from its inulin, a source of soluble dietary fiber that functions as a prebiotic, or food source for beneficial bacteria in the intestines.

In 1769, in Brunswick, innkeeper Christian Gottlieb Förster began manufacturing roasted chicory root and founded a factory to manufacture it in Brunswick and later in Berlin. Chicory is grown and harvested much like sugar beets. The spindle-shaped root is pulled from the ground, washed, cut into small pieces about half an inch in length, kiln dried, roasted, ground and packaged. During roasting, chicory's carbohydrates are caramelized, providing chicory its distinctive dark-brown color and increasing its sweetness.

In 1796, Charles Frances Giraud of Homing introduced chicory as a supplement to coffee in France. Wilhelm Guenter founded the first chicory factory in Germany in 1804. From these humble beginnings, chicory growth and production ballooned. During the 1800s, it was grown and processed in many European countries, with France and Germany leading the pack. By 1856, Germany was the largest producer of chicory coffee worldwide. Wilhelm Bader introduced steam engines, large roasting machines and mechanical processing for milling and roasting chicory.

Much of this growth had to do with Napoleon's elimination in 1806 of coffee imports into much of Europe. When the import ban was lifted, the French and some other Europeans continued to drink chicory as a blend with their coffee. France exported 1.25 million pounds of chicory in 1825 and 16 million pounds in 1840. Today, France remains one of the largest producers of chicory for coffee. Café Du Monde and many other roasters in New Orleans still source their chicory from France (although others buy from Nebraska).

A Rich History

Chicory plant. *From Wikimedia Commons.*

Very likely, French who immigrated throughout the 1800s to France's former colonies introduced coffee-chicory blends to each place. In the first decade of the nineteenth century, approximately 9,000 people moved to New Orleans from the former French colony of Saint-Dominque. Soon, two waves fled France: royalists chased out by the French Revolution and then revolutionaries disappointed with Napoleon. From 1820 to 1900, more than 353,000 people immigrated to America from France, and many of them were drawn to Louisiana because of cultural and linguistic connections.

Coffee and chicory blend, most often served with warm milk, is a traditional New Orleans coffee. As for when coffee-chicory blends began to be drunk in New Orleans, a popular origin myth is that the use of chicory in coffee developed during the Civil War, when coffee importation was severely curtailed and even halted completely for one full year. Thus, chicory extended scarce coffee supplies. Coffee was scarce during the Civil War not only in New Orleans but also throughout the country. People everywhere and soldiers on both sides of the war began using roasted acorns, corn, groundnuts and beets, as well as chicory, to stretch out or substitute for coffee. If this is the way chicory was introduced in New Orleans, many believe thanks go to Henry Lonsdale, a major coffee importer in the mid-nineteenth century.

This origin myth has some holes in it, largest of all is that most chicory was being imported along with coffee. However, ground chicory can last one year, making it possible to use as a coffee extender during short-term shortages and as substitute for longer shortages. But to last as long as the coffee shortage in New Orleans during the Civil War, there must be other explanations.

It is possible homegrown chicory was used. According to Café Du Monde, the Acadians—who became known as Cajuns—came to New Orleans from Canada in the 1760s and brought the taste for chicory in coffee. Also, despite the popularity of the Civil War origin myth, food historians now state that the chicory root—as a supplement or

New Orleans Coffee

Dried chicory root. *From Wikimedia Commons. Licensed under the Creative Commons Attribution 2.0 Generic license.*

replacement for coffee—came to New Orleans from France during the early 1800s. Chicory growth and production, in minor quantities, existed in and around New Orleans. Many immigrants to New Orleans in the 1800s were entrepreneurial. In 1831, new French immigrant Jean Pierre Requirand wrote a Mr. Bousquet in Paris requesting chicory seeds to use, with other plants, to start a business in America. William Dinn advertised in the September 18, 1846 *Daily Picayune* a variety of "superior fresh garden seeds" for sale, including "chicoree [*sic*]."

Additionally, the many Germans who immigrated to New Orleans could have brought chicory with them. About 550,000 immigrants entered the United States through the Port of New Orleans between 1820 and 1860, making it the second-leading port of entry in the United States by 1837. Of those 550,000 immigrants, tens of thousands of German immigrants arrived in New Orleans annually in the 1840s and 1850s. They did not all stay in New Orleans, but a substantial number did. In 1860, approximately 15 percent of the city was German-born or of German descent. Starting with the ban on coffee in Prussia, German women became large drinkers of chicory. They were described as "regular chicory topers," *toper* being a word normally associated with those who drink alcohol to excess. Likely they brought that taste to New Orleans.

After the Civil War, many coffee makers continued to make blends that contained chicory. Chicory was cheaper than coffee and difficult to detect in poor-quality coffee. As early as the beginning of the 1800s in England, grocers, who then supplied a large quantity of ground coffee, were adding chicory to coffee. By 1865, some in Europe had begun to describe chicory as an adulterant during the various debates about how to regulate food and drink.

In the United States, the move toward government regulation of food and drink began in New York in the late 1850s with the "swill milk" scandal. Distillers had to dispose of their waste, and they did this by feeding the mash to old, sick cows. They then milked the cows, added water to increase the milk product. Eight thousand infants died from swill milk. Public outcry led to the passage of the first food safety laws in the form of milk regulations in 1862, the same year President Lincoln established the Department of Agriculture and the Bureau of Chemistry, the predecessor of the Food and Drug Administration.

With this focus on safe food and drink in the latter 1800s, when factories were manufacturing greater amounts, questions arose about the many additives in these foods. Among the products of public concern were milk diluted with water, maple syrup diluted with cane sugar or glucose, spices with added ground wheat and corn and coffee with chicory and other roasted vegetable products. The 1906 U.S. Pure Food and Drug Act states that it is illegal to manufacture any food that is adulterated or misbranded. Adulteration included the removal of valuable constituents, substitution of ingredients to reduce quality and addition of harmful ingredients. Misbranding was defined as making false or misleading label statements. Since most people saw chicory not as an additive but as a substitute that reduced quality or at least made coffee less expensive, coffee and chicory mixtures had to be labeled with a table showing the percentages of coffee and of chicory. Branding was the focus, largely because Dr. Harvey Wiley, a passionate advocate for this law, had stated, "The injury to public health is the least most important question.... The real evil of food adulteration is deception of the consumer."

An early court action based on this law limited C.W. Post from calling Postum, made from roasted wheat bran, wheat and molasses, a "cereal coffee" because it was not a coffee. By similar reasoning, coffee and chicory mixtures had to be labeled with a table showing the percentages of coffee and of chicory. Such branding helped many consumers see chicory as an adulterant. Coffee and chicory blends became a small portion of the coffee market—except in New Orleans, where many prefer the coffee chicory blend, not just to save money, but for the flavor and the tradition. In a city of many culinary traditions—such as crawfish boil, the Sazerac, bananas Foster and freshly shucked Gulf oysters—chicory coffee is one of the most historic flavors.

Others around the country still preferred chicory as a drink, often provided to children since it is caffeine-free. The Tariff Act of 1890 placed a tariff on manufactured chicory but not on raw chicory. As a result, within a short time, about fourteen factories processing chicory put to work about nine hundred people in New York and New Jersey. Others outside New Orleans also love chicory, even if not in coffee. Novelist John Updike wrote in praise to the plant:

> *Show me a piece of land that God forgot—*
> *a strip between an unused sidewalk, say,*
> *and a bulldozed lot, rich in broken glass—*
> *and there, July on, will be chicory,*
>
> *its leggy hollow stems staggering skyward,*
> *its leaves rough-hairy and lanceolate,*
> *like pointed shoes too cheap for elves to wear,*
> *its button-blooms the tenderest mauve-blue.*
>
> *How good of it to risk the roadside fumes,*
> *the oil-soaked heat reflected from asphalt,*
> *and wretched earth dun-colored like cement,*
> *too packed for any other seed to probe.*
>
> *It sends a deep taproot (delicious, boiled),*
> *is relished by all livestock, lends its leaves*
> *to salads and cooked greens, but will not thrive*
> *in cultivated soil: it must be free.*

As Updike must have known, chicory is toxic to internal parasites, such as worms, which has resulted in its widespread use as a forage supplement for farm animals. The chicory root contains up to 20 percent inulin, which has the power to reduce the body's acidity and can be helpful to prevent digestive problems like acid reflux and indigestion. It is used to treat various intestinal problems, including irritable bowel syndrome, constipation, gallstones and gastritis, as well as liver ailments, including hepatitis, jaundice and liver enlargement. It also is used to treat rheumatism, urinary ailments, acne, cellulite, diabetes, eczema and gout. Medical researchers are examining whether inulin can decrease bad cholesterol and triglycerides and, thereby, reduce the risk of atherosclerosis. There also is research into inulin's and chicory's ability to increase calcium absorption and bone mineral density.

A Rich History

However, Dr. Andrew Weil warns that chicory can trigger reactions in people who are allergic to ragweed pollen or sensitive to related plants, including chrysanthemums, marigolds and daisies.

Coffee and Chicory Cookies
Makes 3 dozen

1 cup (2 sticks) butter, softened
1 cup dark brown sugar, firmly packed
2 eggs
2½ cups flour
½ teaspoon salt
2 teaspoons baking powder
½ teaspoon vanilla
½ cup coffee and chicory concentrate

Add ins:
1 cup toffee brittle, if desired, or 1 cup chopped hard coffee candy, if desired
½ cup coffee icing (see recipe below)

Preheat oven to 375 degrees. Place butter and sugar in bowl of mixer and mix until fluffy and lightened in color. Scrape down sides, and then add 2 eggs and mix in thoroughly. Combine flour, salt and baking powder in separate bowl. With mixer on low, add dry ingredients to butter and sugar. Add vanilla and coffee concentrate to dough. Mix again until just incorporated. Add brittle or coffee candy pieces to dough and, by hand, gently stir brittle into the mixture. Chill dough for 30 minutes to an hour. Drop dough by tablespoons onto a cool, parchment-lined cookie sheet, leaving 1 inch of space between cookies. Bake for 12 to 15 minutes until golden brown.

Allow to cool completely before icing. Drizzle icing on top of cookies, or dip cooled cookies in icing. Allow icing to set for at least 20 minutes before putting cookies away.

• • •

New Orleans Coffee

Coffee Icing
Makes ½ cup

1 ¼ cups confectioner's sugar, sifted
2 tablespoons coffee and chicory concentrate

Combine ingredients in small bowl and mix with spoon until smooth. Add more coffee if mixture is too dense to drizzle.

Variation: Using a food processor or coffee bean or nut grinder, grind coffee or espresso hard candies to a chunky powder and stir them into the icing.

Reprinted with permission from NOLA.com | The *Times-Picayune*

7
THE GOLDEN ERA OF NEW ORLEANS

From 1810 until 1840, the population in New Orleans grew from about 20,000 to about 102,000, becoming the country's third-largest city. In 1850, the population was 116,000, and by 1860 (with the annexation of parts of Jefferson Parish (county)), the city had swelled to 168,675. And the population changed dramatically—from a Latin Creole society, composed of people descended from the first immigrants from France, Africa, Spain and Ireland joined by additional French and African Creoles from Haiti, to a heterogenous gumbo with the addition of hundreds of thousands of Americans from the rest of the country and immigrants from most of the existing European countries. Between 1820 and 1860, approximately 550,000 immigrants entered the United States through New Orleans. In 1860, the majority of the white population was foreign-born, with 20 percent born in Ireland or descended from Irish and another 15 percent German. French speakers—the majority of Creoles—were a minority in the 1830s.

The rest of the country was growing as well. Formerly frontier towns like Pittsburgh and St. Louis were now cities, and new frontier towns were beginning all along the Mississippi River's western tributaries. This meant one thing in New Orleans: more trade. That is why these years before the Civil War were the golden age in New Orleans. In fact, the site for the city was chosen because of its proximity to the Atlantic Ocean, both via the Mississippi River and Lakes Pontchartrain and Bourne. While many believe this was because the city provided an ideal port for items coming in from the French colonies both north and south of the city, in Canada and the Caribbean, for export elsewhere, Louise McKinney pointed out that the city fathers also "recognized its strategic geographic importance as a gateway to the riches of North America." Similarly, Thomas Jefferson recognized the value of the geography, calling it "the mighty mart of merchandise brought from more than a thousand rivers…[where] no such position for the accumulation and perpetuity of wealth and power ever existed."

In the beginning, the city's port was largely a depot for goods transported from French and later Spanish lands, awaiting further transport out of the city. Toward the end of Spanish rule, the government recognized the value of bringing goods grown within the Louisiana territory—mostly cotton and sugar—to New Orleans for export. People soon realized that fortunes could be built from storing goods and serving as brokers, while the government amassed income from inspection, notarization and taxation. Don Almonester, a sharp-eyed, wealthy businessman in New Orleans through the Spanish period, predicted in a letter to his wife quoted by Christina Vella, "that as a result of the growth in trade with the rapidly expanding United States, 'property will double in value and our city will resemble Philadelphia in the diversity of the nations who will live here.'"

Commercial travel by water was actually cheaper than by land (Jennifer Jensen Wallach noted that the cost of shipping a ton of wheat dropped 90 percent on canals as compared with roads); however, most water travel was downriver. New Orleans, being the southernmost port of the 2,320-mile Mississippi River, was the natural endpoint for much commercial travel in the United States. The Mississippi watershed includes tributaries that extend into all or parts of thirty-two states and two Canadian provinces between the Rockies and the Appalachians. Small wonder that McKinney dubbed it the "'four-lane' highway of commerce and adventure." Charles Kuralt noted that the mud of thirty-two states and two provinces travels south into the Mississippi River delta, and "500 million tons of [that mud are deposited] there every year. The business of the Mississippi, which it will accomplish in time, is methodically to transport all of Illinois to the Gulf of Mexico."

After the American Revolution, commerce-minded Americans traveled down the Mississippi in flatboats, propelled by oars, or keelboats, moved by a long oar in the center of the craft. Men could help propel the boats from shore, using long poles. They brought agricultural produce from the vast American territory to New Orleans for shipment to ports on the East Coast, Europe and Latin America. In discussing Abraham Lincoln's flatboat journeys to New Orleans, Richard Campanella recorded the size of the port

A Rich History

Keelboats, flatboats and steamboats at New Orleans wharf. *From Wikimedia Commons.*

and the resultant workforce of agents, factors, brokers, lawyers, bankers, and merchants (including traders in enslaved people). He stated, "The port never closed. While late summer and early autumn activities paled in comparison to winter and spring, vessels nevertheless arrived year-round, seven days a week. Wharf action slowed down on Sundays to about one-third normal levels. Nightfall precluded much activity, but lanterns, torches, gaslights, and moonlight allowed shipmen to squeeze additional hours out of their port call." As Joan Garvey and Mary Widmer said, "Levees were lively with peddlers, female vendors, beggars, and machine pitchmen."

Navigation back upriver was difficult and usually required pulling by men or mules. The flatboat men often sold not only their merchandise but also the ballast and the boat itself. These were appreciated in New Orleans; as Garvey and Widmer pointed out, some sidewalks (known locally as *banquettes*) "were made of flatboat gunwale in the 1830s. By the 1850s, some were composed of broad slabs of slate." This slate arrived as ballast on returning ships that had delivered Louisiana cotton and sugar to Europe. Other roads were maintained by chain gangs of convicts.

The steamboat, introduced in 1812, spurred the city's growth. Upriver travel times were greatly decreased; a keelboat trip of several months could be made via steam in less than two weeks. Coffee, as well as other items from South America and goods from Europe and South America, could be shipped upriver to the rest of the United States. In that year, Major Amos Stoddard called New Orleans "the great mart of all the wealth of the Western world." As Ned Sublette pointed out, New Orleans connected, in commerce and communication, "the Mississippi water shed, the Gulf Rim, the Atlantic seaboard, the Caribbean Rim, Western Europe (especially France and Spain), and various areas of West and central Africa." Richard Campanella quoted a statement written in 1829 by Hugh Murray: "There is in fact no part of the world where a fortune may be made more speedily and certainly. There is more employment in every trade than there are hands to execute; even a good tailor may make a little fortune in a few years."

Samuel Clemens, better known as Mark Twain, a nom de plume from his riverboat days, wrote in *Life on the Mississippi*: "It was always the custom for the boats to leave New Orleans between four and five o'clock in the afternoon. From three o'clock onward they would be burning rosin and pitch pine (the sign of preparation), and so one had the picturesque spectacle of a rank, some two or three miles long, of tall, ascending columns of black smoke blended together and spreading abroad over the city."

Steamboat travel had its hazards. One of the worst disasters occurred on November 19, 1849, when the steamboat *Louisiana* blew its boiler. One of the boats next to it was blown fifty feet out of the water. The damage when this boat was "hurled with inconceivable force" included cutting a mule in two and killing "a horse and the driver of a dray to which they were attached," reported that evening's *Daily Picayune*. Also destroyed was a popular coffeehouse, five blocks from the site of the accident, according to Gaspar Stall. Nevertheless, steamboats proliferated.*

The coffee business reflected the larger growth and prosperity. In 1803, according to Martin's *History of Louisiana*, New Orleans imported 1,438 bags of coffee weighing 132 pounds each. All of this was likely for local use. By 1857, coffee importation in New Orleans had grown to 531,236 bags annually. By that time, coffee was being exported from New Orleans to the rest of the country. Per capita consumption throughout the United States had grown from 3 pounds annually in 1830 to 8 pounds by 1859. Some of the increase was due to coffee drinking in the armed services. In 1832, Andrew Jackson replaced rum, whiskey and brandy with coffee in U.S. army rations. During the Civil War, Union soldiers were issued 4 pounds of roasted, ground coffee per hundred rations, sufficient for four to five cups per day.

The best-known coffee importer in the mid-nineteenth century, Henry T. Lonsdale, also was one of the first to export some of the coffee he imported to the rest of America. Born in Brooklyn to English parents, Lonsdale was working on the New Orleans docks as a teenager while his parents were in India. He noticed that many packages were arriving damaged and, having received a sample of jute fiber from his parents, developed burlap packaging. He made a fortune and a name as the "jute-sack baron," "burlap bag baron"

---

* Captain Henry Miller Shreve (for whom Shreveport is named) built the first steamboat that could travel fully loaded upriver through shallow bayous. When he designed his boat, said Gaspar Stall, "he named rooms on board after states; hence the name 'stateroom.'"

or "gunny sack king." In *Cohen's New Orleans Directory* for 1855, his invention, first used to ship shelled corn, is credited with the city receiving two million sacks of "Indian corn" that year. Henry lost his fortune in the Panic of 1837.* But, to quote *Cohen's Directory*, "disasters, however overwhelming, cannot crush a man of true energy."

Lonsdale moved on to importing and brokering other products, chiefly coffee (although gunny sacks remained in his stock). He also knew many dealers throughout the South and West, so he was in an ideal position to promote exportation of coffee from New Orleans. Some of these positive relations may have been due to his ability to provide cash advances: the March 12, 1844 *Daily Picayune* includes a notice that his firm could make "liberal cash advances made on consignments to our friends in Boston, New York, Philadelphia, Louisville, and Cincinnati."

Henry Lonsdale, burlap bag king turned coffee broker. *Reprinted from* Cohen's New Orleans Directory for 1855 Including Jefferson City, Gretna, Carrollton, Algiers, McDonogh.

Lonsdale also produced weekly and annual reports of the coffee trade for the city, detailing amounts imported, exported and stored as of July 1 of each year. These reports show steady growth in New Orleans as a coffee town. For example, coffee imports in 1852–53 totaled 20 percent more than two years earlier. Similarly, stock on hand more than tripled. According to *DeBew's Review*, the total of all coffee stock stored in the United States in 1852–53 was 230,000 bags, more than one-third in New Orleans. The total compared with 100,000 the previous year. The share of this stored coffee in New Orleans could be one reason *DeBew's* said, "New Orleans is the greatest coffee port in the United States."

The coffee trade grew until 1859; Lonsdale's report published in the December 22 *Daily Picayune* that year showed a decrease in bags had been received that year. More ominous: only 6,335 bags were in storage, a decrease of 4,612 bags. In 1862, not a single bag of coffee made it into New Orleans. Lonsdale began reporting again in 1866, when 55,000 bags were imported.

---

* The Panic of 1837 was caused by speculative lending in western states and a sharp decline in cotton prices, among other factors. It caused a recession that lasted until the mid-1840s.

George Westfeldt, founder of Westfeldt Brothers. *Photo by Suzanne Stone, from the Westfeldt Brothers original.*

The late 1850s looked like an auspicious time for importing coffee into New Orleans. So, George Westfeldt, who had started an import business in 1844 in Mobile, Alabama, moved to New Orleans at that time. He had established connections in Brazil, which led to importing coffee. George, whom family members recall was an ambassador for the Swedish monarchy, was joined in 1851 by his brothers Claes and Rhinehold, prompting the firm's name to become Westfeldt Brothers.

Like Lonsdale, the Westfeldts started out by selling their coffee to local grocers and upriver to the new towns being established along the Mississippi. Unlike Lonsdale, descendants of George's have run the company from the 1850s through today. George's son Gustaf became the president. His sons George G. and Thomas D. succeeded him. As the twentieth century dawned, fourth- and fifth-generation Westfeldts served as president. The twenty-first century welcomed the sixth generation, Tommy Westfeldt's daughter Shelby Westfeldt Mills, into the firm as its president; Tommy serves as CEO. The company loves its history and still operates from the same office as the founders.

Shelby said of the business, "What's interesting is that through all these years, coffee remains popular. People love coffee." And in New Orleans, Westfeldts is the largest importer, providing coffee to roasters large and small. The firm's ties in New Orleans run as deep as its roots and as broad as the Mississippi River at Canal Street.

Interestingly, the Lonsdale and Westfeldt family homes are less than two blocks apart on Prytania Street in New Orleans' historic Garden District. At 2523 Prytania Street is the house designed by architect Henry Howard for coffee importer Henry Lonsdale and later owned by, among others, Anne Rice and Nicholas Cage. At 2340 Prytania Street is the oldest house in the district, known as "Toby's Corner," which has been the home of the Westfeldts since 1858.

Despite the growth and prosperity, New Orleans still suffered from the elements and natural disasters. With roads constructed of dust or mud, maintenance was extraordinarily difficult in a city that receives more than sixty inches of rain each year. According to Christina Vella, in 1850,

Westfeldt Brothers' office building, the last remaining in the old New Orleans coffee district. *Photo by Suzanne Stone.*

The New Orleans coffee district in the 1920s. *Illustration* in All About Coffee *by William H. Ukers. From Wikimedia Commons.*

"Gutters along the sidewalks were installed but never cleaned. The city surveyor noted that after only a few months, one new walkway had ten inches of 'green filth' in its gutters, 'just like the sidewalks all over the city.' In summer, every ditch had its scab of hardened excrement." Mel Leavitt added, "The only sewers were open drains, clogged with garbage, refuse, and human waste."

Every year, people suffered and died from cholera, smallpox, malaria and yellow fever. Epidemics, during which the mortality rate could be 60 percent of those who were sickened, occurred frequently, helping make New Orleans one of the nation's deadliest cities. And, the same lack of drainage systems that aided in the spread of disease made the city's streets as treacherous as they had been one hundred years earlier. The city invested $5 million in streets, drains, and banquettes in 1835, but 75 percent of the city remained unpaved after that effort. The February 8, 1850 *Daily Delta* reported, "The rain fell steadily from morning to noon, from noon to night. Streets were mire and sidewalks slippery....Pedestrians knew not the color of their garments, so besprinkled and bespattered with the prevailing currents of mud."

New Orleanians, however, always bounce back.

Greek Revival mansion designed by Henry Howard in 1856 for Henry T. Lonsdale. *From Wikimedia Commons. Licensed under the Creative Commons Attribution 2.0 Generic license.*

Constructed in 1838 for Philadelphia-born wheelwright Thomas Toby, this has been home to the Westfeldts since 1858. *Photo by Suzanne Stone.*

Coffee-Roasted Sweet Potato Dessert Fries Drizzled with Dark Chocolate

2 large organic sweet potatoes or yams, scrubbed and dried*
1 to 2 tablespoons grapeseed oil
1 teaspoon sea salt
1½ teaspoons cinnamon
½ teaspoon fresh ground nutmeg
2 to 3 tablespoons good-quality medium-roast ground coffee (I used decaf so it wouldn't keep me awake)
4 ounces good-quality dark chocolate (I used 70 percent cocoa, but I think the sweet potatoes are sweet enough that I could have used 75 percent cocoa)

Arrange the oven racks so that one is in the middle of the oven and the other one is on the top. Preheat oven to 450 degrees. Prepare two large rimmed baking sheets by lining them with parchment paper or a Silpat mat.

Cut each sweet potato into 1-inch sticks as follows: Using a large chef's knife, carefully cut the ends off. Then cut the sweet potato in half lengthwise. Turn the cut sweet potato on its flat end and cut in half again. Cut each quarter into quarters again. Continue cutting each piece until they are 1-inch-wide sticks. You can either cut the sticks in half lengthwise or keep them long. The short ones crisp up faster, but I am a big fan of long fries. Your choice.**

Place all of the fries on the baking sheets. Add the grapeseed oil and toss to coat the potatoes. Add the salt, cinnamon, nutmeg and ground coffee. Toss well to combine. Arrange the fries on the baking sheets. Make sure the fries aren't touching each other and that the pan isn't overcrowded. This helps the fries to crisp up.

Bake the fries for 20 to 30 minutes. Halfway through the baking time, flip the sweet potatoes and rotate the pan. The fries should be tender in the middle and slightly crisp on the edges. Allow to cool for 3 minutes before removing from the pan. Before the fries are done, break up the chocolate into a microwave-safe bowl. Heat the chocolate on a low power setting 2 minutes at a time until melted. Make sure to stir the chocolate after each heating until it is done. Alternately, you could use a double boiler, stirring frequently.

Transfer the fries to a large plate or platter. Drizzle the chocolate on top of the fries and serve the remainder on the side for dipping.*** Serve the fries immediately or within the same evening. They are best warm out of the oven, but they are still good at room temperature. They do not keep well overnight. I suggest adjusting the recipe amount according to the number of people you are serving. I recommend ½ to 1 whole sweet potato per person.

Notes:
*I buy organic so that I can leave the skin on without needing to worry about pesticides. Leaving the skins on saves me time, adds flavor, and nutrients
**I cut my fries a little larger because I like them to be tender and almost doughy with a slight crisp on the edges. If you would like your fries to be crispier, simply cut them to a ½-inch thickness rather than 1-inch thickness. You may need to alter the cooking time accordingly.
***If you have leftover chocolate, you could toss in some of your favorite nuts and allow to set to create a chocolate bark. Or you could cover the chocolate and reserve for future melting purposes, such as another round of sweet potato fries.

—permission to reprint granted by Emily Koch, recipe at https://robustrecipes.com/coffee-roasted-sweet-potato-dessert-fries-drizzled-dark-chocolate

8

NEW ORLEANS RISES AGAIN

The Civil War impoverished the South, New Orleans and its port included. During the war, the Union naval blockade cut off the port, decreasing all trade by vast amounts. As an 1883 *Times-Democrat* article pointed out, New Orleans received less than 2 percent of all imports in the United States in 1883 compared with 20 percent in 1860, about one-quarter of all bales of cotton in 1883 compared with two-thirds in 1860. Blockade runners based in the Caribbean sneaked in much-needed, high-value goods such as rifles, medicine, brandy, lingerie and coffee to Southern ports. But New Orleans was a particularly difficult port for blockade runners to reach. Successful attempts were cause for great rejoicing in the city, as when a German American of the city "succeeded in running the federal blockade with a shipment of Nuernberg beer."

Apparently, those attempting to bring in coffee were not as successful. Elizabeth Ripley recalled,

> *Every blessed one of us was a coffee drinker, and even before the secession of Louisiana we were weighing and measuring what coffee we had on hand, not knowing where we would replenish our diminishing stock. Governor Manning, of South Carolina, and his wife were our guests at this crisis, and Mrs. Manning showed me how to prepare a substitute for coffee.... The first substitute, which was followed by a store of others, was sweet potatoes, cut, dried, toasted, ground, and boiled. The concoction did not taste so very bad, but it had no aroma, and, of course, no exhilarating quality; it was simply a sweet, hot drink.*

Judging by the lack of coffee reports, there were years when, officially, no coffee at all was received in New Orleans. By the end of 1865, New Orleans was back in business. A notice in the December 30, 1865 *New Orleans Times* stated, "Among the solid exemplifications of the resumption of our foreign trade, we have to note the issuing of the weekly coffee circulars of our old, well-known dealer in the trade, Henry T. Lonsdale." Although coffee was flowing into and out of New Orleans once again, the trade did not surpass that in New York for a number of decades. Quarantines of the port whenever yellow fever reached epidemic proportions (as in 1867 and 1878) and the inadequacy of the port's storage contributed to New Orleans' standing in coffee importation. Before that, the lack of effective connections via railroads was a factor.

The first blow to New Orleans' supremacy as a trade port came from the Erie and other canals. The second, much more serious, was the growth of railroads. When the Erie Canal was built, New Orleans city officials were aware that the city's commercial growth was threatened by its increased traffic, which could connect easily to the northern states' east–west railroads. In January 1830, the Louisiana legislature addressed this concern by authorizing the Pontchartrain Railroad Company to build a railroad from New Orleans to Lake Pontchartrain. This was the first charter for a railroad west of the Alleghenies. In 1831, the four-and-a-half-mile rail line, later known as Smokey Mary, opened from the riverfront to the lakefront town of Milneburg (since annexed into New Orleans).

The growth of the city and surrounding areas had early on mandated the need for additional intercity travel; by 1835, the new cities of Carrollton and Lafayette were connected to New Orleans (into which they were later incorporated) by the New Orleans and Carrollton Railroad. This has become the St. Charles Streetcar Line, the oldest continuously operating car line in America and included in the National Register of Historic Places.

Despite this early start in railroading, continued rail expansion did not occur, in part because the Creoles largely continued to rely on the supremacy of water traffic. The newly arrived businessmen from the rest of America envisioned New Orleans, as Christina Vella asserted, an entrepot of both north–south and east–west exchange. "If the city was to remain the unchallenged port of the Gulf of Mexico, they said, it also had to become a railroad center." But William Henry Sparks, a lawyer who was in practice with New Orleanian Judah Benjamin* from 1852 to

---

* In an April 28, 1855 letter to Samuel L.M. Barlow, Judah Benjamin, who was then a U.S. senator from Louisiana, wrote about the "poor untaught savages of New York" who did not know how to make coffee.

1861, commented on the differences between the Creoles and the "Anglo-Americans," as he called others from the United States who had moved to New Orleans. "The Anglo-American commences to succeed and will not scruple at the means....Moral considerations may cause him to hesitate but never restrain his actions....The Gallic or French American is less enterprising, yet sufficient for the necessary uses of life; he is more honest and less speculative."

In 1860, New Orleans was served by only 143 miles of track. In contrast, by 1850, the 9,000 miles of railroad lines in the United States were mostly in the North and Midwest, which had linked every major city by rail by 1860, according to Salomon Frederik van Oss.

After the Civil War, transcontinental rail service began, first with service from New York to San Francisco. Then, in 1900, the Southern Pacific provided rail traffic from New Orleans through Texas, New Mexico and Arizona into California. As the war demonstrated, rail traffic had many advantages over water traffic: trains could go where no natural river or manmade canal could exist, could travel year-round without concern for weather conditions and were faster than ships. By 1880, New Orleans was served by four railroad lines, and in 1883, the Illinois Central connected to New Orleans. By 1890, railroads had grown to carry about five times more freight than was being transported by water traffic.

Thus, by the 1880s, the South was beginning to recover economically, with almost daily reports in the New Orleans newspapers of recovering cotton crops. In 1882, the National Cotton Planters Association suggested that the 100th anniversary of the first export of cotton be celebrated. Congress passed an act establishing the World's Industrial and Cotton Centennial of 1884. New Orleans would host. The exposition also was intended to boost New Orleans, both economically and by announcing it was back in business, ready for corporate and personal travel. One million people came to the eighteen-month centennial, far less than the hoped-for four million, and it lost $500,000, largely due to mismanagement and corruption. However, the centennial boasted an observation tower with electric elevators and working models of experimental electric streetcars; it was fully lit by five thousand electric lights. One hallmark was the Horticultural Hall, which included a coffee tree.

By then, coffee importation was a growing business in New Orleans. William Ukers reported, from the low of almost no importation during the Civil War, coffee imports reached a total of 337,000 bags in 1893–94 and 514,000 bags in 1900–1901. By 1903–4, slightly more than twice that amount (over 1,000,000 bags) was received, and that was roughly one-quarter of the country's demand. The revival of the coffee trade was due in large part to the coffee firm of Hard & Rand. Recognizing that steamer rates were much cheaper for routes to New York, the firm began chartering steamers for New Orleans trade. Preeminent before that was E.P. Cottraux, who took over Henry Lonsdale's weekly coffee reports in 1880.

By 1880, a number of firms had joined Cottreaux and the Westfeldt Brothers: P. Poursine & Company, Dymond & Gardes, Schmidt & Ziegler, J.L. Phipps & Company, George O. Gordon & Company and Smith Brothers. Of these, only the Westfeldt Brothers remains. Shelby Westfeldt Mills speculated that excellent personalized customer service may be the reason. She explained that Westfeldt will split shipments to as small as one bag, whatever the customer needs. Its niche is small- to medium-sized customers. Also, it buys from just about every country selling coffee, not just Brazil, its original source, and continues its own cupping by mouth to ensure the quality and consistency.

According to the Louisiana State Museum, "One of the most influential firms was J. Aron and Company." In 1898, the firm was founded by Jacob Aron, who had learned the commodities business from an uncle in Chicago. During the city's last yellow fever epidemic in 1905, Aron, with his partner Leon Israel, turned the resulting shortage of coffee (as the port was closed during epidemics) into high profits.

Soon thereafter, Aron moved to New York, leaving his new partner, William B. Burkenroad,* in charge of the business. Burkenroad's son, William B. Burkenroad Jr., began managing the company in the 1930s and stayed until it went out of the coffee business in 1977. In the July 2014 "Freeman Centennial,"† his grandson Robert Bories recalled, "It was a very romantic business—dealing with foreign countries and currencies, shipping the coffee, and trade quotas by producing countries." Bories also described the complexities of coffee brokerage, describing how Indonesian coffee bound for Holland might be sold to an importer in Brussels. During that coffee's voyage, the Belgian might intend to sell to a roasting customer in France. "Meanwhile the price of coffee might have gone

---

* These men remain well known in New Orleans coffee in the twenty-first century. Allan Colley and Tommy Westfeldt both remembered that the Arons and Burkenroads were "fine gentlemen." Reilly's President Jim McCarty said, "J. Aron and William Reily were like this [with two fingers crossed]" and added, "He was the sharpest businessman I've ever known in my life." Additionally, William Ukers stated in his obituary for Aron, "Aron was the first in New Orleans to issue coffee market forecasts, which were uncanny in their exactness. His opinion was eagerly awaited by the entire industry."

† Published at the 100th birthday of the A.B. Freeman School of Business at Tulane University.

down, or another shipment of that coffee turned out below standard, so the Marseilles roaster might resell at a loss to the original buyer in Holland. We, in New Orleans, speculating that coffee might have a big market in the United States in several months, have already contacted the Holland agent, and the coffee that was originally destined for that country now lands in New Orleans."

The day after J. Aron Company discontinued its coffee business in 1977, ten former employees started the International Coffee Corporation (ICC), working in the same offices and desks vacated by J. Aron. Now home to the St. James Hotel, the Magazine Street side of the building included a block-long arcade, known as the Banks Arcade. That is where J. Aron New Orleans operated. At various times, the Leon Israel Brothers and the Cargill Corporation operated from that space. ICC has since relocated to New Orleans suburb Metairie.

ICC was started by William Madary Jr. and now includes his daughter Marie, who worked with him at the J. Aron Company. It is headed now by William "Will" Madary III and Matt Madary. Will joined after a long history in the communications industry and acknowledged, "This is a unique business." He elaborated, explaining that he had come from a world where deals included lengthy legal negotiations. He joined ICC, and his dad would come back from a lunch at Bon Tons with a bunch of cocktail napkins in hand. "He'd hand me one, saying, 'I sold this much coffee to this person' and so forth." The company is today, as Matt said, "value buyers." He recalled his dad saying, "You can't sell from an empty cart." So, they buy coffee that meets various customers' profiles and have it available. Again, to quote their father, "You make your money around the cupping table." The brothers love the business. Will called it a "gentlemen's business": "deals made on the phone, everyone lives up to their word, and your competitors are good customers of yours." Matt enjoys learning something every day. "The product comes from the soil and changes season to season, year to year."

Leon Israel, meanwhile, joined his brother Samuel Israel. They soon owned a coffee growing business in Brazil, giving them more control over reliability, quality and prices (in large part because they did not have to constantly negotiate with growers). Leon's son, Leon Israel Jr., was born in 1906, and after learning the business from his father, he became a coffee trader and expanded the operations to New York. By the 1970s, the company expanded and dealt not only in green coffee, but also sugar, rubber, cocoa, grain, steel, gold and currencies.

Will (*left*) and Matt Madary. *Photo by Suzanne Stone.*

A branch of Leon Israel & Bros. Inc. continued to do business in New Orleans. During World War II, the company was run by Merryl Silverstein Israel. Before that she was a champion golfer who started winning city championships in 1933. She played with many other golf champions, including Ben Hogan, Jimmy Demaret and Babe Didrikson Zaharias. She also played golf and sold war bonds with Bob Hope and Bing Crosby. After her first husband, Sam Israel Jr., died, she married his cousin, Jack Aron, from the coffee importing Arons. Perhaps not surprising in a town known for its small number of degree of connections, Mrs. Aron also lived in the Garden District, just one block from the Westfeldts, in a famed Italianate home on First Street.

These importers largely sold the green coffee they imported to coffeehouses and grocers, both within New Orleans and upriver. Soon, however, they recognized the growth of coffee consumption throughout the country and the increasing trend—at least outside New Orleans—for consumers purchasing roasted and ground beans instead of raw, green beans. The industry was spurred by two inventions: the paper bag and a coffee roaster that could be used in commercial production.

A Rich History

In 1876, in New Orleans—where people vastly preferred to roast and grind their own coffee to ensure quality and taste—only four New Orleans coffee importers were roasting: Shaw's Louisiana Coffee and Spice Mills, Ruliff, Clark & Company, R. Poursini & Company and Smith & McKenna (later Smith Brothers). Between 1876 and 1900, four more were added: American Coffee Company, New Orleans Coffee Company (which later joined the American Coffee Company), Southern Coffee Polishing Mills and Cage & Drew (which later became the Louisiana Coffee Mills). The American Coffee Company was founded in 1890. Its first product was French Market Coffee. Later, it also roasted and sold brands used at two of the city's biggest hotels, St. Charles and Monteleone, plus brands for two universities, Tulane and Loyola. Honeymoon and French Opera were sold nationally. Coffee had taken its place in the city's rising prosperity.

William B. Reily started as a grocery clerk and then a wholesale grocer in nearby Monroe, Louisiana, where he developed his expertise in roasting coffee, an increasingly popular product, for his customers. Moving to New Orleans in 1902, Reily started a company to roast, grind, package and distribute canned coffee. This company developed Luzianne coffee and chicory. His friend Jacob Aron joined the Reily Board of Directors in 1906, about when the company added tea to its product line. By 1932, William B. Reily & Company was distributing Luzianne coffee and chicory blend and tea to commercial customers in Louisiana, Mississippi, Alabama and Georgia, as well as parts of Florida, the Carolinas and Virginia. With son William B. Reily Jr., the Reilys started the Standard Coffee Company, which delivered coffee products directly to consumers' homes.

William B. Reily, founder of Reily Foods. *Photo by Suzanne Stone and reproduced with permission of Reily Foods.*

According to Reily president Jim McCarthy, after World War II, soldiers in the Reily Company distribution area returned home with a desire to drink coffee without chicory, and others had been won over by national brands. Reily found its market contracting, and the company focused on diversifying. In 1946, Reilly Foods acquired and built coffee roasting factories in Baltimore and, in 1964, bought JFG Coffee in Knoxville, Tennessee. Further diversification came when in 1968 Reily bought CDM Coffee and eventually

Left: Coffee can with Café Du Monde label; *Right*: Coffee can with Luzianne label. *Photos by Suzanne Stone and reproduced with permission of Reily Foods.*

Blue Plate mayonnaise from Blue Plate Foods. In 2009, the American Coffee Company was acquired, bringing the eponymous French Market Coffee into its realm.

Like Reily, H. Norman "Cap" Saurage started as a grocer. He operated a country store in 1919, selling his own brand of coffee, which he named Community Coffee out of appreciation for his community of friends and the customers he served. From this beginning, one hundred years later, the Saurage family is still selecting, grinding and roasting coffee in Baton Rouge, Louisiana, and selling to wholesale customers and restaurants. In 1995, the company began CC's coffee shops in New Orleans and quickly opened franchises across the region. The coffeehouses are still run by the Saurage family but as a separate business.

In 1923, the company was trucking roasted coffee beans from New Orleans and blending, grinding and packaging them in the converted barn behind Cap's house. When the first industrial coffee grinding mill was brought in on a wagon, the load was too tall to get in the barn door. Employee Julius James dug ruts in the ground for the wagon wheels so the grinder could be brought inside.

H. Norman Saurage III remembered when his father (known as HN) decided that the company should roast its own coffee beans. In 1941, Cap and HN went to the coffee trade district in New Orleans. "Coffee, sugar, and cotton were traded [in the New Orleans Board of Trade] by open outcry in two large trading pits set down into the main wooden floor." Outside the building, they saw people in the green coffee business carrying "their little open sample trays, filled with a half-pound of unroasted green coffee beans, to the roaster so that the roaster's buyer could examine and grade the coffee." Mr. Schanzer, of R.E. Schanzer Company, their supplier for roasted chicory, told them he had a new Jabez Burns "Jubilee" one-bag roaster he would have delivered to Community Coffee for the original price of $750. That was the start of roasting. The family said that despite these achievements, "HN's greatest asset was his taste buds. He was an exceptionally good coffee taster."

With roots this deep in the New Orleans coffee community, it came naturally to the Saurages to step in during the aftermath of Hurricane Katrina. After all, as third-generation Community Coffee owner Donna Saurage said, her husband, H. Norman Saurage III, "always used to say everything we do has to be as good as our coffee." The CC's on Magazine Street became the gathering place for the community to discover information and updates. Staff from around the areas would set up "virtual coffeehouses," serving coffee from backpacks. Donna said the company began opening coffee shops because they are an extension of the company name, *community*. Coffee shops are "places where people want to gather and share news. And what better time than after a disaster to help people gather together." This experience helped launch other disaster relief efforts. The company has served over 1.7 million cups of Community® coffee to relief efforts since 2005. Also, as part of the family values, Community Coffee provides about 2.5 percent of its pretax income to charitable, socially responsible programs regionally, nationally and internationally.

Donna Saurage, third-generation Community Coffee owner. *Photo by Suzanne Stone.*

Though not a charitable donation, the company also helped a young Jim Henson. From 1957 into the early 1960s, the company ran some ten-second television commercials. The producer was Henson Associates. As H. Norman Saurage III recalled, "At the time Jim Henson was trying to get started financially to launch his Sesame Street Muppets on TV.... The Company's Muppet ads on television were pretty popular."

Clearly, New Orleans was firmly established in the country's second wave of coffee production and drinking, just in time to take advantage of the third invention, vacuum packaging, that made the coffee most people knew through the first three quarters of the twentieth century. In the 1940s, HN began selling Community Coffee in vacuum, or brick, packs. The removal of air from coffee tins resulted in fresher beans. Now, coffee moved from being sold unroasted and unground to the housekeeper and to local or regional grocery stores for processing there to being sold as roasted, ground, packaged coffee to retail outlets from sea to sea and from the Gulf to the northern border. From that time to now, as Tommy Westfeldt noted, some of their customers "roast, grind, blend and serve their coffee in a coffee shop; others roast, grind, and blend and package or send on for packaging and shipping to specialty, grocery, and larger stores."

This change in the coffee business paralleled what was happening throughout the city. In 1870, there were 544 factories; by 1890, that number had grown to 2,152. Among these factories were ones roasting coffee. John Magill noted that by the early 1900s, "About 90% of coffee sold in New Orleans was commercially prepackaged, allowing producers to sell in neighboring states."

Coffee firms actively worked to improve the port in New Orleans. First was a push to move control from private interests to the public sphere. On July 9, 1896, the Louisiana legislature created the Board of Commissioners of the Port of New Orleans, commonly known as the Dock Board. Two other improvements occurred to boost New Orleans as a premier coffee importing city: public health efforts that stopped the regular outbreaks of yellow fever epidemics, during which the port would be closed, and the development of a publicly owned belt railroad, providing all major railroads uniform access to the port. When the rails for this "public belt railroad" were laid, on July 1, 1905, James Porch,* then an inaugural member of the Belt Commission, stated in his keynote that New Orleans was the twenty-second seaport worldwide with this advantage and the only one in the United States.

As commercially produced coffee proliferated, so did complaints of adulteration. Mark Pendergrast quoted New Yorkers in the 1870s, who said that "pure coffee is rarely to be had except in private families where the head of the house attends in person to the preparation of the precious

---

* Porch also played an important role gaining materials shipped through New Orleans for the construction of the Panama Canal, opening traffic via that route for the city.

cup," and "In the City, veritable coffee has become extinct." While chicory was the most common additive, many other products were added to coffee, including bran, bread crusts, brewery waste, brick dust, coal ashes, dog biscuits, gooseberries, kola nuts, lentils, linseed, sand, sassafras and wood chips. In New York, it was discovered that coloring was being added to Guatemalan and Venezuelan coffee to make it resemble Java; the coloring included arsenic and lead.

As noted in chapter 6, coffee was one of the specific food and drink products included in the 1906 Pure Food and Drug Act. Earlier federal efforts to regulate food safety focused on butter and margarine (1886), salted pork and bacon (1886) and meat inspection (1891). Harvey Wiley, MD, was responsible for the larger focus. As chief chemist in the U.S. Department of Agriculture in 1902, he studied the effects of a diet consisting in part of preservatives. These studies spurred interest in a federal food and drug law. Wiley led this campaign, giving him the title of "Father of the Pure Food and Drugs Act."

Coffee continues to grow as an industry in New Orleans. According to John Magill, by 1966, "coffee made up more than one-third of all imports through the Port of New Orleans," and in "1995 New Orleans imported 27.8 percent of the nation's coffee and outranked New York as the Americas' leading coffee importer." New Orleans is home to the first silo warehouse in the United States. In 1989, Allan Colley, the third generation of Dupuys to manage the Dupuy Group, expanded the operations to a former glass bottle facility that included a silo. Colley was aware of the coffee silo facilities in Europe and the cost savings that could be obtained with them.

So, he thought, "why not?," and in 1992, he changed the way coffee was stored in the United States: in polypropylene "super sacks," rather than the much smaller Lonsdale-invented burlap bags. But it has not changed how Colley measures the coffee in his warehouses: he still thinks and talks in terms of 132-pound bags. Each of the silos in that Dupuy facility in New Orleans East contains "20,000 bags." His daughter, Janet Dupuy Colley Morse, says "2,640,000 pounds." The square silos are divided into cells that allow for different coffees to be stored separately. Most coffee is delivered to Dupuy in twenty-foot containers, and each silo can hold sixty-six of those containers. Some coffee is still delivered in standard 132-pound bags, and Dupuy serves small and large customers.

John Dupuy founded Dupuy Storage in 1936, opening the first warehouse on South Peters Street in the heart of the coffee trade business in New Orleans. By 1949, the firm had moved to a larger facility and opened a

Paradoxically, right across the street from the Westfeldts, at 2343 Prytania, is a home designed by James Freret in 1872 for sugar baron and distiller Bradish Johnson, who was one of the New York city distillers involved in the swill milk controversy, which was the impetus for pure food regulation in New York. *Photo by Suzanne Stone.*

second green coffee silo facility in Jacksonville, Florida, in 2005. After Katrina, a warehouse opened servicing the Port of Houston. Today, the Dupuy Group also has facilities in South Carolina. Dupuy provides the basic services of storage and delivery for green bean importers and roasters that it has for eighty-plus years: receiving coffee on behalf of a customer, roasting a sample for tasting and then—if the customer is satisfied that what has arrived is what was ordered—storing the coffee and delivering it upon

A Rich History

Coffee companies store coffee at Dupuys from all over the world. *Photo by David Feldman.*

request. Dupuys has offered roasting services since the beginning when John Dupuy acquired a Jabez Burns roaster from a tenant.

Janet explained that the firm also has added "value-added services." Other services include coffee sampling, blending and upgrading (cleaning, separating heavy foreign material from good coffee beans (destoning), sizing and color-sorting). The value-added services came as a result of events that occurred during the various eras of coffee growing and processing. Allan Colley recalled his father telling about shipments where "the bags containing coffee were loaded in the front, and that's what we would sample, but the bags in the back contained bricks, to make the weight." All of this ensures, according to Janet, that Dupuys is "a partner with the coffee importers and roasters."

In fact, Westfeldt Brothers, still a customer, was Dupuy's first client: Janet confirmed a story told by her longtime friend Shelby Mills that the first invoice from Dupuy to Westfeldt was not for coffee storage but for some cachaça, hard liquor made from sugar cane, brought in from Brazil. Allan added, "If you know the coffee business, you know liquor consumption is a big part of it. The coffee business was very fraternal, and once the business was done in

The Bon Ton Café, meeting place of New Orleans Coffee Men. *Photo by David Feldman.*

the morning, it was time for lunch, which was a three-martini lunch, as far as I can tell." He also remembers one coffee man who did business from the Bon Ton Café, the watering hole for the local coffee industry.

Today, New Orleans is the largest coffee import city in the country; Ned Hémard stated that approximately one-third of all coffee imported into North America arrives in the New Orleans port and that "some dozen local roasters, including Folgers, import an average 250,000 to 300,000 tons of coffee beans annually through the port." According to Charlie Schmitz, it was the port's share of coffee importation that caused Procter & Gamble, when it purchased Folgers, to move the processing operation to New Orleans. Here they developed the "Folgers crystals." Charlie described standing on the six-story tower watching the "instant coffee being sprayed into the nitrogen and floating down into the furnace." Folgers Coffee joined the J.M. Smucker Company's family of brands in 2008.

In addition to being the home of the largest coffee roasting plant, New Orleans is the site also of Silocaf USA LLC, the largest automated silo plant in the world fully dedicated to green coffee processing. Silocaf, established in the 1990s, is part of the Pacorini multinational company, which provides logistical services for a broad range of commodities and general cargo.

Honey Cake
Makes 2

Permission granted by Sheryl Title, who said, "This recipe is from my Aunt Dora Teles. She was the best 'Jewish cook' I ever met. She cut no corners. She died at the age of 95 in about 2008."

8 medium eggs
A little cream of tartar (about ¼ teaspoon)
1 ¼ cups sugar, sifted once
2 cups honey (buy a 32-ounce jar)
¾ cup Wesson oil
1 teaspoon each of the following flavors: vanilla, almond, sherry (can add a little more of this), rum and brandy
Allspice and cinnamon (about a teaspoon each)
5 ¼ cups flour (only Swansdown or Softasilk), sifted twice
2 ¼ teaspoons baking powder
1 ½ teaspoons soda
¾ cup strong black coffee
Some whiskey (about 2 tablespoons)

Preheat oven to 350 degrees. Line pan with wax paper, allowing paper to extend over sides. Separate eggs. Put yolks in a large bowl, as all ingredients will be added to this. Add cream of tartar to whites. Beat whites until they stand up. Add about ½ of the sugar and continue until stiff (like for chiffon cakes). Beat yellows, add to sugar until very light and lemon color (light yellow). Add honey and beat well. Add oil with flavorings and cinnamon. Add flour, baking powder and soda alternately with coffee. Fold in stiffly beaten whites with the whiskey. Fold whites only a little at a time. Bake for 1¼ hours. Turn off oven and let sit for another 10 minutes. Take out of oven and remove from pan when cake is cold.

Notes:
The longer the yolks beat, the better the cake will rise. Beat 'til it rises, 5–10 minutes *at least*. When you add flour and coffee, turn beaters down lower, so flour won't sprinkle. Afterward, turn beaters higher. After pouring cake into pans, stand the wax paper on the sides up, cuz the cake may rise over the sides.

DO NOT OPEN OVEN TIL IT IS TIME TO REMOVE. After 1¼ hours, you can open the oven…press cake with finger. If it springs back, cake is done. DON'T STICK WITH KNIFE. While the cake is in the oven, it is like a baby sleeping—don't slam the door or drop anything on the kitchen floor. They say I'm nuts, but I think this has a tendency to make the cake fall.

Note to her granddaughter, Sheryl: "Next *yontiff* [holiday], all of you will send us some of your honey cake."

9
SHOPS IN THE FRENCH MARKET

While coffee importing and exporting and roasting, grinding and packaging increased, people in New Orleans continued to drink coffee, at home and away, all day, every day. By the middle of the nineteenth century, in addition to the coffeehouses centered in the old city, now known as the French Quarter, individuals continued to vend throughout the city and have stands in all the markets, the oldest and best known of which is the French Market. According to Nancy Brister, in the early 1900s, every New Orleans neighborhood had its own market, totaling thirty-two public markets. The French Market was originally established in 1779.

The French Market today hardly resembles the market of that day or even earlier trading posts that served the first citizens. Redesigned in 1913, revamped in the 1930s and again in the 1970s and run according to twenty-first-century market and cleanliness standards, it does not even resemble the market of the 1880s, as described by Will Coleman (and recounted by Louise McKinney): "From the ceiling hang endless ropes of spider webs, numberless flies, and incalculable dirt. The stalls are deeply worn by the scraping process; in some yawn pits, apparently bottomless; and lastly the floor of the market is not at all clean, but covered with mud and dirt from the feet of its patrons."

Somehow, the patrons managed to not only come in droves but also enjoy themselves. Lyle Saxon, Edward Dreyer and Robert Tallant recalled that Sundays at the French Market included "not only the unique variety of characters, but a contagious spirit of festivity, as if everyone were on holiday instead of merely shopping for the traditionally large Sunday dinner." Items for sale then included—in addition to the coffee that had been available since the late 1700s—meats, fish, fruits, vegetables, "parrots, monkeys, mockingbirds, canaries, alligators, mousetraps, rat poison, toothache cures, crockery, and all sorts of notions and knick-knacks."

The second half of the nineteenth century saw the expansion of coffee stalls into coffee stands in the French Market. Their pull was as irresistible as during the previous century. Lyle Saxon recalled his first visit to New Orleans as a young boy, going with his grandfather to a coffeehouse "tucked away between the stalls of fruit and vegetables" where they drank hot, black coffee together while "around them the market men drink coffee and discuss the affairs of the day."

A December 26, 1896 article in the *Daily Picayune*, "Christmas Morn in the Market," described the festive atmosphere on Christmas Day as last-minute shoppers thronged the market before rushing off to mass at the cathedral. The author wrote, "The coffee stands did a business in the morning eclipsing that of any bar in the city. Coffee appeared to be immensely popular, as did chocolate, but it did not begin to compare with the coffee business." According to Lafcadio Hearn, the coffee vendors "are acknowledged as the elite of the market society." He described them as adjustable: "condescending to the vegetable sellers, urbane to respectful customers, and pitying to visitors maybe from the country who appear not to understand the difference between *café au lait* and *café noir*."

All the coffee stands, then and now, are leased from the city. In 1894, the "Virginia Kitchen" coffee stand at Decatur and Ursulines was for sale, and the ad noted a daily rental fee of $3.50. A letter to the editor of the *Daily Picayune* remonstrated against a proposal to sell market stalls to the highest bidders, pointing out that the coffee stalls pay the most. Other news articles described murders and robberies in coffee stands and sales of stands throughout the market, including one in 1884 of an unnamed coffee stand at Decatur and St. Ann. This is the corner on which Café Du Monde sits.

The more well-known coffee stands in the French Quarter "were celebrated by people from all walks of life in the late 1920s," according to the *Times Picayune*'s James Karst, in a review of newspaper articles from the time. An item in a June 10, 1928 issue reported, "Sweet young things in evening dress rub elbows with unshaven hucksters in overalls; dowagers sit down beside yeggmen; cake eaters, gamblers, debutantes, artists, taxicab drivers and tourists from all parts of the world mingle and fraternize together."

A Rich History

Inside the coffee stand at the head of the French Market, circa 1880s. *Photograph by Suzanne Stone from original at Café Du Monde.*

According to Jay Roman IV, owner of Café Du Monde today, the original stand that opened in this location in 1862 was not named Café Du Monde, but once it started serving the Café du Monde brand of coffee, it soon adopted that name for the stand. The Café du Monde brand was started by D.H. Hoffman, who worked for coffee broker E.P. Cottraux until going into business for himself, founding the Southern Coffee Mills in 1887. Paul Vargas said that the brand formerly served at the coffee stand at that site was French Market Coffee, one of the brands of the New Orleans Coffee Company, Ltd. The company used that location as part of its advertising.

Today, Café Du Monde serves coffee, other drinks and beignets. The coffee includes chicory (the exact percentage is a trade secret) and can be ordered black, with or without sugar and with milk. The café au lait is made the traditional way—brewed coffee added to milk heated, never boiled, in a separate vessel. The drink is mixed only when the order is placed. Non-coffee drinks were added in the 1980s, when the store expanded its locations. In 1984, the Louisiana Pavilion of the World's Fair hosted in New Orleans was upriver from the market and is now the site of the Riverwalk

Marketplace. Café Du Monde planned to expand into that space. About the same time, the developers of the Esplanade Mall being built in Kenner, Louisiana, approached Roman and, eventually, at a dinner at Mandina's, presented a lease drawn up on a cocktail napkin that offered five years on very favorable terms, including his ability to end at any time. All the machinery was purchased and awaiting the opening of Riverwalk, so Jay Roman decided to give the Kenner location a try. He chose to add soft drinks, which would be expected in a mall. Orange juice had been added in the early 1980s after a four-year debate. The new stand was successful, so new machinery was needed for Riverwalk. Gradually, milk was added to the menu, and in 1988, iced coffee was introduced to the café.

French Market coffee can label, showing the coffee shop at the head of the market. *Photograph by Suzanne Stone.*

The first Café Du Monde can seat four hundred and employs forty wait staff. Customers may notice that many of the staff appear to be of Vietnamese heritage. Jay explained that he was asked in 1975 by Catholic Charities to help with some refugees from Vietnam arriving in New Orleans. Many of these newcomers felt comfortable with the atmosphere at the café, reminding them of the French-style coffeehouses with which they had grown up. Many of the current staff are third-generation descendants of those first immigrants.

Jay described the way his family came to own Café Du Monde. In 1941, his grandparents met and married when they each worked for United Fruit in Honduras and returned to the United States for health reasons. His grandfather H.N. Fernandez opened the Fernandez Wine Cellar on Decatur Street, across from Café Du Monde. Fernandez became friendly with Fred Koeniger, who owned the iconic coffee stand. When Koeniger was ready to sell, Fernandez was ready to buy. He maintained the stand as Koeniger had, serving coffee and beignets.

The other major coffee stand in the French Quarter over the last century and a half was Morning Call, founded in 1870 by Joseph Jurisich, an immigrant from the Austria-Hungarian Empire. Operated by his descendants until December 2018, Morning Call was second only to Antoine's in length

A Rich History

Left: Jacques Roman, who says he eats beignets every time he cooks them at Café Du Monde; he tastes one from each batch to ensure the high quality; *Right*: Jay Roman IV, owner of Café Du Monde. *Photo by Suzanne Stone.*

of operation under the ownership of a single family. Current owner Robert F. Hennessey[*] explained that his mother married Joseph's grandson after a divorce, bringing Robert, David Michael and their sister, Karen Meyer, into the family. The boys worked at Morning Call from their teenage years on. Alvin Jurisich disinherited his children from his first marriage and ensured with legal documents that his second wife and her children would inherit the coffee shop.

Morning Call was located at the other end of the Market from Café Du Monde until 1974, when it moved to the suburb of Metairie. Until then, the two stands served almost as bookends of the French Market. For almost a century, the two competed for the loyalty of local and visiting lovers of café au lait and beignets. However, in some ways, the two shops supported each other. Jay Roman remembers going over to Morning Call to borrow ingredients they had run out of and providing the same to Morning Call

---

[*] Robert says they are related, "in some way," to David C. Hennessy, a police chief in New Orleans who was assassinated in 1890. The acquittals and mistrials following his murder resulted in the lynching of eleven of nineteen Italian Americans who had been indicted. Ultimately, the United States paid about $2,200 to each family of the eleven victims.

Postcard looking down river on Decatur Street, with Morning Call café with its signature sign shaped like a giant coffee cup. *From Wikimedia.*

in their temporary shortages. While locals may still have their favorite, for visitors, there cannot be too many coffee shops in New Orleans.

Remembering when Morning Call was in the lower French Market, Erroll Laborde wrote, "Morning Call was a happy place that was as much a visual experience as a place for libation. Inside was a classic marble counter with a wooden frame lined with light bulbs. Waiters, wearing white jackets and paper service caps, would hustle the orders. There is no better aroma than that of *café au lait* and beignets. The essence of Morning Call was its own perfume."

Robert Hennessey stated that the move to Metairie was a result of changes in the French Market that eliminated the parking at Morning Call. "Roadside service was the largest part of our business," he said. His stepfather "did not think people would pay $1.00 to park for a 20 cent cup of coffee." The move started as a success: loyal customers followed Morning Call to the "Fat City" section of Metairie in such quantities that "we had to install heaters for people standing in line."

Since 2012, Moring Call was located in the Casino Building, the structure also known as the Timken Center, in City Park. As Erroll Laborde noted, Morning Call is no longer near the Mississippi River, but now borders the last remaining section of Bayou Metairie and is open twenty-four hours a day, just as it was in the French Market. Also, the design—with tile floors, marble counters, big steel coffee urns and an arch of bare lightbulbs—recalled the photos of the original Morning Call. When it moved to this location, the shop added what the previous restaurant had on its menu—classic New Orleans fare such as gumbo, jambalaya, red beans and rice—plus ice cream, beer and Irish coffee. The Hennesseys are seeking a new location for Morning Call.

Robert Hennessey pointed out the differences between the two old cafés: first, Morning Call made its coffee the old French drip way, using old pots and cloth filters made by his sister. They could make only five gallons at a time, resulting in fresh coffee being made constantly. The staff also poured each cup of café au lait by hand. According to Robert, "There's an art to it." They were also able to tailor each cup to the customer's preference. Except, the only coffee served was a coffee-chicory blend. Second, the waiter served each cup of coffee by hand, able to balance as many as six cups and saucers at a time. Again, Robert said, "It's an art." Finally, the beignets: at Morning Call, the recipe included sourdough batter, which Robert insists "makes the beignets lighter." In addition, the cooks used the beignet cooking techniques established by Joseph Jurisich: dough was rolled and cut by hand, resulting in unique beignets. If the customer wanted, the beignet dough could be scored, resulting in "beignet fingers." And, finally, the beignets were served unsugared. "We let you put on your own sugar. That's part of the charm of the experience," according to Robert. At Café Du Monde, those in the kitchen sift the sugar onto the beignets in such quantities that people are warned not to wear black when visiting the shop.

Beignets were not always part of the coffee stands' menus. Lafcadio Hearn described breakfast in the market coffee stands as including beefsteak, mutton chops, soft-boiled eggs or chicken. The earliest mention of a doughnut being sold at a coffee stand occurs in a news article in September 1871, describing serious scalding injuries to coffee stall "keeper" Mrs. Barbarucci, which were incurred while she was "boiling a pot of grease" with which to make doughnuts. But since their start, these confections have been a draw.

Beignets at Café Du Monde. *Photo by Suzanne Stone.*

They were on the menu at Martin Brother's Coffee Stand and Restaurant, best known for

Beignets at Morning Call. *Photo by Suzanne Stone.*

inventing the "po' boy" sandwich for striking streetcar workers in the 1920s. It opened in 1919 as a French Market stall serving coffee, doughnuts and lunches. Brothers Clovis and Bennie Martin had worked as conductors on the New Orleans streetcars. When the streetcar workers went on strike in 1929 the Martin brothers wrote a letter in support of the strikers to the president of the Division 1904 union, promising to provide "a free meal to any members of Division 194." Their bakery supplier, Gendusa's, modified the loaf from a "torpedo" shape to one that had a uniform width through the entire three-foot loaf.

BEIGNETS

James Karst explained that while coffee may have been the main menu item at the coffee stands, the larger attraction was the doughnuts. As the *Times Picayune* reported on August 27, 1927,

> *They aren't anything that an ordinary doughnut is. The reason is that they are better. There is just about as much comparison between the so-called doughnuts at the Morning Call and the usual true species of doughnut that everybody knows as there is between a Lindbergh and a mudcat. To eat the doughnuts at the Morning Call is to remember them a lifetime. They are that good. And they aren't made quite so good anywhere else in the world.*

In 1927, Louis Gillette of Café Du Monde told the *Item* that a tourist offered $250 for the doughnut recipe, but he wouldn't provide it for that or any other amount.

In a 1961 interview with *People Magazine*, Truman Capote (who worked on his first novel while living in New Orleans in 1945) described some of his early morning activities:

> [Capote] *pauses en route at a temporal abode: the doughnut café in the renovated version of the old French Market. During his long nights as a young writer, Truman would wander over at 4:00 am and watch the truckers and vegetable farmers. "Wow, did this used to be a sexy place," he says. "The truckers used to try to lure me to the backs of their trucks." Did he yield? "Well," Capote giggles, "sometimes."*

Guests to New Orleans today can see the doughnut, as they were called until 1958, being made at Café Du Monde. The cottonseed oil (a Louisiana product) is kept boiling in vats near the machinery used to make the beignets: the dough is rolled out and then scored. Skilled cooks then gather a few of the beignets and toss (or "flick," as Jay described it) the dough into the oil. The tossing is necessary, as that separates the flour, providing the lightness

This page: Making beignets at Café Du Monde. *Photos by Suzanne Stone.*

of a beignet. This is a skilled task, and Jay and his son, Jacques, have taken their turns, learning the proper way to make the doughnut.

The word *beignet* may come from the Celtic *bigne* ("to raise") or from the Spanish name for yeasted fritters, *buñuelos*. According to food historian Cathy Kaufman, the French beignet appears in France in the sixteenth century, during Mardi Gras celebrations, and she proposed that "Mardi Gras beignets may have their origin in the medieval Islamic dish luqam al qadi, a version of which appears in the Baghdad Cookery Book of 1226." According to this thesis, the Moorish courts in Andalusia influenced Spanish cooking and later integrated into other European cuisines. Kaufman argued that "what ultimately makes luqam al qadi so tempting as the origin of the Mardi Gras beignet is the use to which devout Muslims put the little pastries: they were a traditional part of the meal breaking the Ramadan fast. Sephardic Jews also used sweet fritters called bimuelos (Jewish dialect for the Spanish buñuelos) to break the Yom Kippur fast."

Some today argue that the beignets found in New Orleans are more like the Spanish fritter than the French one. Cuisine in the city was influenced by both the French and Spanish in the eighteenth century, so the New Orleans beignet's origins may never be known. The popularity is not in doubt.

If beignets are not available, cream puffs might substitute for breakfast.

Coffee Cream Filling for Cream Puffs

1 cup whole milk
½ cup sugar
3 tablespoons flour, or 1 tablespoon cornstarch
Pinch salt
2 large egg yolks or 1 large egg, lightly beaten
1 teaspoon vanilla extract
2 teaspoons instant coffee

Place milk, sugar, flour and salt in a 3-quart pan. Mix well and cook, stirring constantly, over low heat until mixture thickens. Stir in egg yolks and bring to a boil. Cook on low, stirring constantly, 3 minutes. Stir in vanilla and coffee. Chill thoroughly before filling cream puffs.

—recipe reprinted with permission from Nancy Tregre Wilson's *Mémère's Country Creole Cookbook*

10

BEYOND THE FRENCH MARKET

Although the French Market has operated almost continuously since its founding in 1789, thirty-plus other neighborhood markets have diminished, even closed, over the years. Coffee was moving outside the neighborhood markets during the twentieth century, which dawned rosily for New Orleans. In 1901, the city celebrated the centennial of becoming American; it was held two years early so President William McKinley could attend. One of the biggest accomplishments was the New Orleans Sewerage & Water Board hiring A. Baldwin Woods to improve the city's drainage. Soon, the swamps in the middle of the city were drained, allowing for expansion, and an underground sewage system installed, with drains pulling out the fetid water and refuse. Such drainage reduced the incidence of yellow fever. The 1905 epidemic was the last in the city, thanks to efforts by the state and city boards of health. By 1909, the city had sufficient pure water for drinking and adequate removal of sewage. In 1927, surveying began for the Bonnet Carré spillway, to be used to divert the Mississippi River when flood threatened.

The lights that had electrified the Cotton Exposition now were lining Canal Street and were promised for every home. Skyscrapers of five to eight stories began to punctuate the landscape. City Park now included a golf course, a mechanical carousel and a race track (soon moved to its present location nearby). In 1911, the Delgado Museum (now the New Orleans Museum of Art) opened.

However, the original city—the French Quarter—was vastly different than it had been in 1860. Poverty stemming from the Civil War caused the Quarter's buildings to become dilapidated. In the early 1900s, two city blocks were demolished for the new Louisiana Supreme Court. In 1917, at the secretary of the navy's command, whorehouses were evicted from Storyville, only to move into the Quarter. In 1915, the old St. Louis Hotel was demolished by a hurricane, and in 1919, the French Opera House was destroyed by fire.

The decay of the Quarter resulted in rock-bottom rents that were perfect for poor artists and writers. If one could not afford to travel to Montmartre, one moved to New Orleans. According to Scott Dechamps, these bohemians joined students seeking "poetry and intellectual vibrancy in the coffee shops and salons" and became active in efforts to save the French Quarter. Sherwood Anderson, fresh off his literary success with *Winesburg, Ohio*, first came to New Orleans in 1921. Anderson and his second of four wives moved to New Orleans in 1924. They took up residence in the Pontalba Apartments on Jackson Square. There the Andersons entertained Carl Sandburg and Edmund Wilson and allowed a young William Faulkner to sleep on their floor.

Prohibition became the law of the land in 1919. Nevertheless, coffee was not the only beverage being served in the French Quarter during Prohibition. "New Orleans did seem to have heard of [Prohibition]," remarked one contemporary. Five-term New Orleans mayor Martin Behrman summed up the general attitude: "You can make it illegal, but you can't make it unpopular." Beer, supplied directly from the breweries through under-street hotlines, continued to flow freely in the bars, which added a "winy-beery smell to the Quarter's rich, spicy aroma of roasting coffee and seafood." William Faulkner was known to drink alcohol heavily. "Sherwood Anderson recalled [Faulkner owned] an overcoat with additional pockets sewn in to carry [bottles of alcohol]." Another of their set "once saw him bring beignets home from the French Market and eat them for breakfast with a glass of corn liquor." The nation's number one Prohibition enforcer, Izzy Einstein, was in town only thirty-five seconds before making a bust. Einstein asked his cab driver where "he could cure his thirst." The driver reached back with a drink. Einstein cuffed the driver and invoked his usual lament, "There's sad news here." (In comparison, it took Izzy twenty-one minutes to find liquor in Chicago and St. Louis, seventeen in Atlanta and eleven in Pittsburgh.)

Civic-minded women living "uptown" spearheaded efforts to revive the French Quarter culture and save the buildings. Elizabeth Werlein, who moved to the Quarter in the 1920s, founded the Quartier Club and the Vieux

A Rich History

Carré Property Owners Association, an early French Quarter preservation organization. Louise Nixon was the first president of the Le Petit Theatre, a new organization presenting plays in the Quarter. The Arts and Crafts Club, with 75 percent female membership, was one of the most important cultural groups in the 1920s French Quarter. It was first housed in the Green Shutter, a popular spot for writers and artists and for the progressive women working on French Quarter preservation.

By the end of 1921, the Green Shutter also housed a coffeehouse. The *Times Picayune* heralded its opening as the revival of the "old coffee house." Here, the newspaper said, one could drink "the best of New Orleans coffee" and eat waffles or biscuits. There, Lyle Saxon wrote, as quoted by John Shelton Reed, one could find both "artists in smocks discussing this business of life as they sip their coffee in the courtyard" and "a sprinkling of 'uptown' people who have come to see just what these artists are up to." Among the artists were the building's owner, Martha Gasquet Westfeldt (married to coffee importer George Westfeldt), who had her kiln in the courtyard and a pottery workroom above. Guest speakers addressed groups at the Green Shutter. Famed journalist Dorothy Dix urged women to enter business in January 1922.*

The Green Shutter also was one of the first locations for a movie location in New Orleans: in 1922, the Whitman Bennett Company filmed a silent picture in the Quarter, with some scenes in the patio and in the courtyard of the Green Shutter. The *Times Picayune* reported that the movie was *Rose of Sicily*, but it was released as *Fair Lady*. The Green Shutter was only blocks away from the first permanent, for-profit movie theater in the United States, the Vitascope, which opened on Canal Street in 1916. New Orleans would become the "Hollywood of the South" by the end of the twentieth century. More than two hundred movies and TV shows have been shot in and around the city.

Saving the Quarter was not the only progressive cause championed by women in early to mid-twentieth century New Orleans. Martha Westfeldt's sister-in-law, Kitty Monroe Westfeldt, influenced others to become active in highlighting and opposing improper campaign finances and tactics during the 1930s.

Outside the French Quarter, Lyle Saxon told of travelers in the 1920s commenting on "the coffee houses tucked away in corners" across Canal

---

* Dorothy Dix started her career when she was hired at the *Daily Picayune* by Eliza Jane Nicholson, the country's first female newspaper publisher. She went on to become America's highest-paid female journalist by her death in 1951.

Street, in the financial sector. Saxon also said that "French drip-coffee is the favorite legal beverage of the men in New Orleans. And it is no unusual thing for a business man to say casually: 'Well, let's go and get a cup of coffee,' as a visitor in his office is making ready to depart. It is a little thing perhaps, this drinking of coffee at odd times, but it is very characteristic of the city itself. Men in New Orleans give more thought to the business of living than men in other American cities." Many popularize this as the beginning of the coffee break, although the term was not used for a few more decades.

Historians claim the coffee break originated with immigrant women in Stoughton, Wisconsin, who, in the late nineteenth century, took midmorning and midafternoon breaks from their work to check on children and perhaps imbibe some coffee. During the late 1940s, the New Orleans–based Delta Steamship Lines, a large coffee transporter and cruise line, advertised midmorning and afternoon coffee in its elegant onboard salons. The term *coffee break* did not enter our lexicon until 1952, when a Pan American Coffee Bureau advertisement recommended consumers to "Give Yourself a Coffee-Break—and Get What Coffee Gives to You."

Coffee exchanges and coffeehouses—except the French Market stands—were on the decline, but restaurants were expanding. One of the country's first restaurants, Delmonico's, opened in New York in 1827. The first restaurant in New Orleans, Antoine's, which opened just thirteen years later, is still operating today and owned by descendants of Antoine Alciatore's. The Old Coffee Pot opened in 1894 and served from that time to early 2019 dark French Roast New Orleans coffee with chicory and traditional calas cakes, the yeasted fried rice fritters made with leftover rice, once obtained only in one's home or from the street vendeuses. The famous rice fritters were a favorite for those seeking breakfast at the Old Coffee Pot. The restaurant is in an 1829 building (some say one of the brick walls survived the devastating fires of 1788) with a courtyard and attached two-story outbuilding (often called a "dependency") where enslaved people were housed. Like many buildings in the Quarter, it was once a business and residence.

In the 1880s, Dr. Etienne Deschamps had his dental practice on the second floor, fronting St. Peter Street. Dr. Deschamps was among the first to experiment with modern methods of pain reduction, and he was obsessed with finding the hidden treasure of the pirate Lafitte brothers. He believed that his "hypnotic-magnetic" abilities, used with chloroform, could help him discover the treasure. He also believed at least one of the young daughters of his friend, Jules Deitsh, a new immigrant from France, would be the person who would reveal the location of the booty when he used chloroform and hypnosis to mesmerize her. Both girls visited him almost every day after school, and he used chloroform on both on January 29, 1889. The younger girl became ill and refused the chloroform the next day. Her older sister drank it both days and died of an overdose on January 30, 1889. Dr. Deschamps's lawyer proffered an insanity defense, one of the earliest attempts in the United States. It was to no avail. Dr. Deschamps was executed for murder in 1892. Later, the building was bought by a young couple who opened it in 1894 as the Old Coffeepot. The last owner, Dustin Palmisano, and his staff often caught a glimpse of a small girl near the location of the former dentist's office. The restaurant was sold in February 2019 and plans to reopen by fall 2019.

Leah Chase worked at the Old Coffee Pot when she finished high school in New Orleans. She recalled many of the customers ordered the same breakfast every day. One ate only cinnamon rolls and coffee. One man always ate toast and chicory coffee. Another ate nothing but waffles and coffee. One woman's waffles must be cooked, but not brown, "which took some special doing." And there was the man who ate only vegetables every day for lunch. Today, at Dooky Chase's, Leah's daughter-in-law comes in, carrying her coffee cup in her hand—coffee remains that important in New Orleans.

Around the same time, newer immigrants were opening coffeehouses. George D. Zibilich immigrated from Duba, Croatia, in 1874. He fished oysters, a favored trade among Croatians, who pioneered the cultured oyster business in Louisiana. About a year later, he opened a coffee stand with Frederick Bautovich at St. Ann and Dumaine Streets. He left that business and started a grocery, which first was the Penny Post Coffee House. Zibilich left the coffee and grocery business in 1916 to found a chain of movie theaters in New Orleans.

Many people were turning to lunch counters in pharmacies and the new drugstore chains. The most popular in New Orleans was Katz and Besthoff. Every K&B had a soda fountain and served its signature nectar soda (a pink drink flavored with almond and vanilla). But the breakfast menus started with chicory coffee and house-made biscuits, a longtime favorite meal to start the day in New Orleans.

Coffee was getting extra-special treatment at some of the oldest restaurants. Café brûlot, the hot brandy-based cocktail, originally was created at Antoine's sometime after 1910. It can be found at many old-school fancy Creole restaurants. This tableside coffee presentation is like bananas Foster, but much more intricate.

Dooky Chase's Restaurant. *From Wikimedia Commons. Licensed under the Creative Commons Attribution–2.0.*

By the 1960s, coffeehouses in New Orleans served that generation's bohemians, also known as beatniks, and anti–Vietnam War and civil rights activists. Lee Harvey Oswald frequented the Ryder, a well-known coffeehouse, in the summer of 1963 before it closed later that year when the building it was housed in was sold and demolished. That same summer, some of its alumni founded a new coffeehouse, the Quorum, which soon drew attention from the New Orleans Police Department (NOPD). Scott Ellis said, "This meeting place of many cultures was, perhaps, not as political as the surveilling NOPD thought it was.…The never-ending quest for authenticity led many fans of folk music to these clubs where they might dig a performance by renowned Mississippi blues artist Jewell 'Babe' Stovall." Nevertheless, Sharon Stallworth Nossiter reported that the shop was busted in 1964 for "offenses apparently no greater than playing bongo drums, reciting bad poetry, and mixing with people of other races."

Mixing with people of other races was a crime during much of the twentieth century in New Orleans. Dooky Chase's restaurant was "one of the only public places in New Orleans where mixed race groups could meet to discuss strategy for the local Civil Rights Movement," as stated on the restaurant's website. Blueprints for many of Dr. Martin Luther King's sit-ins were mapped out in Dooky's, where civil right leaders of both races gathered, without any arrests ever being made. Reminiscing recently, Leah said her mother-in-law, as well as the rest of the family, believed in treating people well, and that people would treat you well in return. So, for decades, whenever police patrolled the streets near Dooky's, Leah's mother-in-law had freshly made sandwiches and would call out, "*Bébé*, sandwiches are ready for you."

A Rich History

Glazes and Sauces for Ham, Chicken and Beef

Luzianne offered recipes for its coffee and chicory. First, it suggested basting a ham with black Luzianne coffee and chicory, which would make "famous Southern dark gravy." Two recipes for glazes for hams also were offered:

Add 1 tablespoon of honey to 1 cup of black Luzianne coffee and chicory.

Add 2 teaspoons of Luzianne Instant Coffee with Chicory to your favorute glaze mixture.

For a glaze for chicken, the recipe was to add ½ to 1 teaspoon of Luzianne Instant Coffee with Chicory to ½ cup of chili sauce.

Adding ½ cup of black Luzianne coffee and chicory to ½ cup of cooking wine "can turn on ordinary beef stew into a gourmet dish."

—reprinted with permission from Reily Foods

11
COFFEE'S THREE WAVES

By David Feldman

For all but a sliver of coffee's history, a cup of coffee was a do-it-yourself endeavor. You acquired green coffee beans, cleaned them, roasted them, ground them, brewed them and, finally, served the coffee. Coffee involved legacy knowledge passed down from mother to daughter, coffee implements that had developed over centuries and time. Coffee time in Ethiopia, the cradle of coffee, evolved into an extended social and ceremonial occasion. Village politics and gossip passed back and forth among the guests as they snacked. The hostess, enacting this thrice-daily tradition of hospitality, produced the sights, sounds, aromas and anticipation of what, for the Ethiopians, is and was a transformative experience. Each guest is served three cups: *abol*, *tona* and *baraka*. The first is for pleasure, the second for contemplation and the third is a blessing upon the gathered. That's how it was for the first 1,200 years or so. You did it yourself or went to the coffeehouse.

During the past 160 years or so, three overlapping waves of change have transformed the American experience of coffee. Trish Rothgeb explained, "First Wavers made it their mission to increase coffee consumption exponentially.…They revolutionized packaging and marketing of coffee. Air-tight cans, pre-portion packs, and Juan Valdez were their ideas." The Second Wave, with origins in the 1960s, began, as Rothgeb recounted, when "someone turned us onto coffee origins and roasting styles. We looked to the wine industry for inspiration in defining goals and strategies. We started destination shops with small roasting operations and fine tea selections."

After Word War II, Americans were introduced to the social experience of coffee and new coffee drinks like espresso and cappuccino made with better beans. Think Peet's and Starbucks. "With the third wave, production and marketing take the back seat, and the product takes center stage," explained Bradford Lowry. Tim Castle, a thirty-year coffee veteran, wrote, "3rd Wavers devoted unprecedented resources to sourcing....They also worked hard to improve quality controls at all levels both on the side of roasting and preparation of brewed beverages."

The First Wave introduced ready-for-the-pot coffee and ready for-the-cup instant coffee at affordable prices. In 1864, while Union soldiers were issued four pounds of coffee a month and Confederate soldiers and most of their folks at home did without, Jabez Burns invented a revolutionary coffee roaster. The roasting "cylinder" is permanently suspended over the firebox. A chute in the rear loads beans into the roaster, and a gate in the front allows the beans to discharge. Two hand-cranked spiral flanges in the roaster keep the beans moving and, when the gate is opened, empty the roaster. Burns wrote in his patent application (US 44704A), "Coffee can be introduced into the cylinder and discharged therefrom without stopping its motion or removing it from its bearings, and that by this arrangement cylinders of a much larger caliber can be used and much more Work accomplished."

John and Charles Arbuckle, wholesale grocers in Pittsburgh, bought Burns roasters. They patented a glaze "for the purpose of retaining the aroma of the coffee, and also act as a clarifying-agent when the ground coffee has been boiled in water," according to the Letters Patent. They developed and patented machinery to weigh coffee, dispense it by the pound into paper bags and seal and label the bags. Arbuckle's included a peppermint candy in each pound and premiums redeemable "for all manner of items including handkerchiefs, razors, scissors and wedding rings, everything a cowpoke or pioneer might come to need," according to thewildwest.org.

Arbuckle's was the first to brand, promote and sell its coffee nationally. The Homestead Acts of 1862 and 1866 opened the way for massive westward expansion. More than 10 percent of the land area of the country, over 270 million acres, was given away free to more than 1.6 million often immigrant homesteaders and land speculators. Arbuckle's glazed and packaged coffee went west with the homesteaders. Arbuckle's Ariosa brand was the original "Cowboy Coffee." Shipped in Arbuckle Brothers crates containing one hundred airtight one-pound packages, "the new coffee was an instant success with the chuck wagon cooks in the West who were faced with the

A Rich History

Left: Jabez Burns No. 12 Mill, used by Community Coffee to grind coffee from 1926 through 1970. Burns explained in his patent application that "the coffee can be introduced into the cylinder and discharged therefrom without stopping its motion or removing it from its bearings." *Photographed by Suzanne Stone at Community Coffee and reprinted with permission from Community Coffee.*

Right: Jabez Burns from early 1900s. *Photographed by Suzanne Stone at Community Coffee and reprinted with permission from Community Coffee.*

task of keeping Cowboys well fed and supplied with plenty of hot coffee out on the cold range," recounted *True West* magazine. The peppermint candy attracted a steady supply of coffee grinders. "Some of the toughest Cowboys on the trail were known to die for the opportunity of manning the coffee grinder in exchange for satisfying a sweet tooth." The 1890 census declared there was no longer a geographic line in the country beyond which there were fewer than two people per square mile. The frontier was closed. America's Manifest Destiny was realized. Arbuckle Brothers coffee became known as the "Coffee that Won the West."

Fast forwarding to 1900, the Hills brothers of San Francisco, who sold coffee beans to the California prospectors during the gold rush of 1849, introduced vacuum packaging to protect coffee beans from air and moisture. They promised that their "Highest grade Java and Mocha Coffee would KEEP FRESH FOREVER IF THE SEAL IS UNBROKEN." Shortly after, Folgers vacuum packed roasted and ground coffee. Coffee was now available ready for the pot already roasted, ground and vacuum packed for freshness.

New and better ways of brewing coffee came on the market. James H. Mason of Massachusetts registered the first U.S. patent for a coffee percolator in 1865. Percolators boil water in the bottom that rises up through a tube and percolates down through the coffee. Electric percolators came to market during the 1920s. Italian Luigi Bezzera patented the first commercial "espresso" machine in 1901; the Tipo Gigante forced hot water and steam under pressure through the coffee grounds. The coffee was brewed quickly, hence the name "espresso machine." In 1908, German housewife Melitta Bentz fashioned and patented a coffee filter from her son's school blotting paper. The company she founded is credited with the first drip coffee maker. The general trend was to brew better coffee faster with less mess.

Sartori Kato introduced instant coffee tablets at the Pan American Exposition in Buffalo in 1901, and George Constant Washington marketed Red-E Coffee, the first mass-produced "instant coffee," in 1909. Coffee was now ready for the cup. You didn't even need a coffee pot.

National brands like Maxwell House, named after a Nashville hotel, and Chase and Sanborn waged expensive national marketing campaigns throughout the last quarter of the nineteenth and first half of the twentieth centuries. Direct marketing and print advertising gave way to revolutionary new innovations: radio and TV. Chase and Sanborn Coffee sponsored *Major Bowes Amateur Hour*. In 1932, Maxwell House Coffee's *Showboat*, named after the hit 1927 Broadway play, premiered on radio. While *Major Bowes* traveled from city to city, *Showboat* was mythical, totally a creation of radio. The show garnered a huge audience, many of whom wrote to request tickets for the *Showboat* when it docked in their town, according to Mark Pendergast.

The Goldbergs, developed by writer-actress Gertrude Berg, premiered as a daily radio show in 1929 and became a hugely popular television series from 1949 to 1956. "The heartwarming show depicts a lively Jewish family living in New York City: the dutiful children, Rosie and Sammy; Jake, the hot-tempered husband; old-world Uncle David; and, of course, the ever cheerful and gracious Molly (Gertrude Berg). Joined by their extended family and neighbors, the Goldberg house consistently overflows with joy, laughter, and love," according to the UCLA Film and Television Archive. Molly even did the commercials. Looking through her window at the audience, she comforted them that they could drink as much Sanka decaffeinated coffee as they wanted because "they left the sleep in," recounted Mark Pendergast.

A Rich History

The United States became the largest importer of South American coffee in the world by the middle of the twentieth century. Almost all of it was shipped through the Port of New Orleans. By the end of the 1970s, a third of the imported coffee, some 200 million pounds, was Robusta from Brazil processed into instant coffee and freeze-dried instant coffee. In 1972, Vincent Marotta and Samuel Glazer brought to market the first automatic drip coffee maker for home use, Mr. Coffee. Ironically, as instant coffee sales were exploding, people bought forty thousand Mr. Coffees a day throughout the 1970s, with Yankee Hall of Famer Joe DiMaggio as spokesman.

The First Wave had its pros and cons. On the plus side, it revolutionized the packaging and marketing of coffee. But there also was a lot of bad coffee being marketed. Bad coffee "generally came in cans in the North and paper bags in the South, was roasted light, always pre-ground, and not very good tasting but very economical for the average family to have in the pantry for everyday use," according to Donald Schoenholt, who founded the Specialty Coffee Association of America in 1983. "You could always tell the bad stuff as its only descriptive labeling said something as, a blend of the world's finest coffee," he added.

Bad coffee, though, wasn't the only driving force behind the nascent Second Wave. A few pioneering individuals were in "the vanguard of the new coffee business that was being born in the tumult that was America's reawakening to good food in the wake of The Great Depression and a World War," wrote Schoenholt. Avant-garde Americans were learning about and coming to appreciate "specialty" wines and cheeses with their appellation contrôlée designations and grading systems. Analogous systems would much later be applied to specialty coffee.

Alfred Peet, perhaps more than any other person, was responsible for America's nascent interest in food, wine and coffee. In Peet's *New York Times* obituary, Korby Krummer wrote, "He was the guru of everyone in the gourmet coffee revolution. He was the big bang. It all started with him." Alice Waters, whose Berkeley, California restaurant, Chez Panis, pioneered "farm-to-table" cuisine, credits Peet with introducing her to quality coffee. "Everybody was drinking coffee that came out of a can," said Waters. "But Alfred was a purist rooted in the European tradition. He taught us a new way to look at food, wine, and coffee—paying attention to the preparation, the ritual, and understanding how the beans and ingredients were grown."

Peet was born in 1920 in the Netherlands. His father was a coffee wholesaler and roaster. After stints working for tea companies in London and Indonesia, Peet immigrated to the United States in 1955. In 1961, he opened Peet's

Coffee in Berkeley. "At the time, America had a reputation, internationally, as having coffee that tasted like dishwater," said Jim Reynolds, who started at Peet's in 1984. Peet biographer Jasper Houtman repeated a famous Peet quote, "I came to the richest country in the world, so why are they drinking the lousiest coffee?" Clark Wolf, a restaurant consultant, credited Peet with "almost single-handedly helping the American consumer appreciate the dark roast blend."

Alfred Peet's legacy was carried on by three college friends: Jerry Baldwin, Zev Siegl and Gordon Bowker. They opened Starbucks in Seattle in 1971. They bought their tea and coffee beans from Peet's. Baldwin learned to roast green coffee from Alfred Peet. The concept of "specialty coffee" as articulated by Erna Knutsen was still years in the future, but Peet's and the original Starbucks were the precursors.

Erna Knutsen gave a name and definition to the craft Alfred Peet, the Starbucks founders and a few other pioneers had been developing over the preceding twenty years. The concept was quite simple: "special geographic microclimates produce beans with unique flavor profiles, which she referred to as 'specialty coffees,'" explained Ric Rinehart. "Underlying this idea of coffee appellations was the fundamental premise that specialty coffee beans would always be well prepared, freshly roasted, and properly brewed" to extract those unique profiles.

Knutsen started as a secretary at a coffee brokerage. Her eye-opening coffee moment came when she tasted, quite by accident, a coffee from a small Indonesian coffee grower. Though she became America's first female green coffee buyer, the male buyers in her company would not allow her into the roastery or the cupping room. She finally gained access and ended up buying the company and renaming it Knutsen Coffee.

Howard Schultz joined Starbucks in 1982 as retail operations and marketing manager. On a trip to Italy, he became enthralled with the coffee culture of Italian espresso bars. After proving the concept at a Starbucks in Seattle, he went on in 1984 to found a chain of espresso shops called Il Gournale. He bought his coffee from Starbucks. Howard Schultz envisioned people all over the world drinking good coffee in what he termed "the third place," after home and work. In 1985, he bought Starbucks, and the rest, as they say, is history. "Starbucks is an example of a hyper–Second Wave company. They helped introduce the words 'latte,' 'French Roast,' and 'cappuccino' into consumers' vocabularies—not to mention their daily lives," said Trish Rothgeb. Schultz married the social experience of coffee with better coffee and new-to-Americans coffee drinks. For their part, consumers, according to Trish Rothgeb, wanted "to know the origin of their coffee and understand the unique roasting styles of what will now be called 'specialty coffee' beans. This knowledge added to the enjoyment of coffee as an experience, rather than just a beverage."

The Specialty Coffee Association and the Coffee Quality Institute, founded in 1996, developed rigid standards, based in part on the wine model, to assess and maintain the quality of specialty coffee from farm to cup. But unlike wine, which, hopefully, only gets better in the bottle, coffee can degrade in quality if not cultivated, processed, transported, stored, roasted, ground and brewed to exacting standards. A Q grading system evaluating coffee on a 100-point scale, like wine, was developed. Coffee rated at 80 points or above is considered specialty coffee. Since 1996, the Coffee Quality Institute (CQI) "has worked to improve the quality of coffee and the lives of people who produce it" through educational programs.

Nicholas Cho described coffee's Third Wave as "letting the coffee speak for itself." Cho elaborated, "During the first two waves, we appreciated coffee for what it gives us; caffeine, a hot beverage to sip and enjoy a conversation over, a drink to modify with sweetener, dairy (or non-dairy) creamers, syrups, whipped cream, etc. The Third Wave is about enjoying coffee for what it is."

The late Jonathan Gold, Pulitzer Prize–winning food critic, most succinctly summed up the three waves of coffee:

> *The first wave of American coffee culture was probably the 19th-century surge that put Folgers on every table, and the second was the proliferation, starting in the 1960s at Peet's and moving smartly through the Starbucks grande decaf latte, of espresso drinks and regionally labeled coffee. We are now in the third wave of coffee connoisseurship, where beans are sourced from farms instead of countries, roasting is about bringing out rather than incinerating the unique characteristics of each bean, and the flavor is clean and hard and pure.*

In the following pages, you will meet some of the passionate people in various New Orleans neighborhoods who are devoting their lives to putting a truly memorable cup of coffee, often artistically decorated, in front of you.

12
COFFEE IN NEW ORLEANS TODAY

New Orleans Neighborhoods

Like many old cities, New Orleans is composed of many unique neighborhoods. And coffee can be found in almost all of them. That is in part because many are located on Magazine Street, which winds its way through six neighborhoods: Central Business District, Warehouse/Arts District, Lower Garden District, Garden District, Irish Channel and Uptown. A walk or drive through the six miles will bring one to many bars, cafés, restaurants, fine art galleries, clothing shops, jewelry stores and gift stores featuring uniquely New Orleans merchandise, as well as many specialty coffeehouses.

Past Uptown, where St. Charles turns onto Carrollton Avenue, is the Carrollton neighborhood. Carrollton was developed in 1833 as a separate town and annexed by New Orleans in 1874. It has long been ethnically mixed, home to free people of color before the Civil War, joined by immigrants from Germany and Ireland. Home to Tulane and Loyola Universities, Carrollton boasts two "main streets" with some of New Orleans's funkiest stores: Oak Street and Maple Street.

The French Quarter, the original city, is now a special neighborhood, surrounded by the next three neighborhoods in the city. The second neighborhood, originally the *Faubourg* Saint Mary and then the American Sector, is known today as the Central Business District and is next to the

Warehouse/Arts District. This is home to many businesses, the city's government and consulates from Mexico and France. It also is home to the Dryades Market.

The third neighborhood is the Marigny, developed from the plantation of Bernard de Marigny, and once the home to longshoremen and factory hands. Today, it, along with neighboring Bywater, is a vibrant arts and music scene. The fourth neighborhood is the Tremé, developed from Claude Tremé's plantation that served as an early neighborhood for free people of color. It also housed Storyville, New Orleans' red-light district from 1897 to 1917, where many say jazz started.

Another early neighborhood is Algiers, across the Mississippi River. In the 1700s, this was the holding place for Africans who had survived the voyage across the ocean where they could recover before being transported across the river to be sold. It also was a holding area for the Cajuns who moved here in the 1760s, after expulsion from Acadia. Integrated into New Orleans in 1870, Algiers offers a three-mile-long levee for walking and biking,

One neighborhood that predates New Orleans is *Faubourg* Saint John, built along the Bayou Saint John, on the Esplanade Ridge. The area was a Native American trade route, and travel via Bayou Saint John into Lake Pontchartrain and then the Gulf of Mexico was one of the attractions to sieur de Bienville. French trappers and traders settled in this area, already home to Native Americans, by the end of the seventeenth century. The area was incorporated into the city in the nineteenth century. Today, it contains many parks, including City Park; architecturally significant homes, including the Pitot House; and museums, including the New Orleans Museum of Art, plus restaurants and coffeehouses.

Most other New Orleans neighborhoods were developed only after the 1913 design of the Wood Screw Pump by Tulane professor A. Baldwin Wood to drain the "backswamp" and cope with the drainage problems of New Orleans. That "backswamp" became Lakeview, Gentilly and Mid-City. Canal Street bisects Mid-City, which is a racially diverse, middle-class neighborhood with a few businesses, the Orleans Parish Criminal Court and restaurants, coffeehouses and bars that rely heavily on local clientele. Just south of Mid-City is Gert Town, a former manufacturing district and now home to the studios of television station WVUE.

A Rich History

PJ's

Phyllis Jordan moved to New Orleans in 1977 from Des Moines, Iowa. Needing to be employed, she was aware of the success a friend in Des Moines had with a combination bookstore and specialty coffee shop. She also knew how much she enjoyed going there every day for conversation with her friend. With a background in social work, Phyllis appreciated the open atmosphere that allowed people to meet up and converse regularly. After moving, she paid her friend $500 "to come down and tell me how to do it." In 1978, she opened PJ's Coffee on Maple Street. This was first a retail shop, but "after 18 months I realized I was starving, so I changed it to a coffee shop." She found a coffee maker for "only $75.00, which made the decision easy."

Beyond the attraction of the socializing afforded in coffee shops, Phyllis appreciated that the drink was something that just about anyone could afford. It is an inclusive item, attracts everyone. In 1982, one Friday, her friend called to say she was going out of business and offered to sell Phyllis her roaster. The timing was a little off. Phyllis was broke, and her wedding was the next day. The friend replied, "Give me $100/month for two years." And Phyllis was married and in the roasting business. First, she had to find a warehouse, unpack and put together her roaster and learn how to use it. She called the manufacturer, who said he could help her for $1,000. He wrote a letter stating that she was in her bind because "the seller, a woman, had not taught her how to use it." Well, that comment ended any thought Phyllis had of working with him, so she managed to learn what she needed to without his help.

PJ's was such a hit in a city that loved coffee that in just ten years, she had opened three coffee shops. Phyllis credits her knowledge of the nascent specialty coffee business, largely in the Northwest, for the success—that and her own desire to establish places where people would want to gather, similar to Howard Schultz's "third place." No other coffee shop in New Orleans was inviting people to come in and stay for a while, without continuing to spend money. As Poppy Tooker said, "Phyllis Jordan eschewed the term 'coffeehouse.' At the time, that evoked images of dark, smoky places frequented by 'beatniks.' [She] imagined a sunny place that would serve as a neighborhood hub, welcoming moms and children, students and professors, encouraging them to linger over coffee and conversation."

Phyllis thinks that two more factors—her being a nonnative in New Orleans and being a female entrepreneur—contributed to her success.

PJ's roaster. *Photo by Suzanne Stone.*

Being new to the city, Phyllis was not wedded to the traditions so beloved in the Crescent City. But her roots are deep. She added, "You don't put down deeper roots in a new city than with a bank loan." She pioneered the use of cold brew coffee, and PJ's still uses the cold-drip process she developed. She recalled in an interview with Poppy Tooker about the annual meetings of the National Coffee Association in the mid-1980s, where the long-standing members decried, "Young people want a cold drink." Again and again, Jordan stood up and said, "'Yes, I'm doing cold coffee in New Orleans and it's doing quite well.'" But no one paid any attention for a long, long time.

After the third shop opened, a friend asked Phyllis to get involved in this exciting adventure. She decided it was time to explore a new world to conquer. She began franchising her coffee shops. The first PJ's Coffee franchise location opened in 1989. And this was another learning experience for Phyllis. As she said, "I care about the quality of the coffee in each store, and a franchise owner cares about his or her own profit." Those goals can be—but are not always—completely compatible. In 2008, PJ's was purchased by New Orleans natives and brothers Paul, Steven and Scott Ballard of

Ballard Brands. Phyllis learned from her early franchising experiences to insist that her business model and philosophy be part of the business, as long as it bore her initials. PJ's Coffee continues to use only the top 1 percent of premium arabica beans. Employees travel around the world to hand-select the best coffee beans.

ORLEANS COFFEE

By David Feldman

Bob Arceneaux has been in the coffee business in New Orleans for more than thirty years. He likes to say his Orleans Coffee Company in Kenner, Louisiana, just outside the city, is "New Orleans' first specialty coffee roaster." Some of Bob's wholesale accounts have been buying from him for more than twenty years. Some of his mail-order customers are second generation, "which," he said, "is pretty neat." Growing up in New Orleans, he only drank the local commercial coffee. "Nothing else passed my lips. That's all my momma brought home." His eureka coffee moment came less than a decade after Erna Knutsen first coined the term "specialty coffee" in 1978.

The Specialty Coffee Association of America (SCAA) was founded in 1982 and established standards, practices and a grading system. Erna Knutsen, a "feisty little woman," according to Bob, worked her way onto the trading floor of a coffee brokerage. Bob credits her with being the "fairy godmother" of specialty coffee.

"I was in the wine business and somebody said you ought to go and check out this place called PJ's." Phyllis Jordan, a transplant from Des Moines, Iowa, had opened a coffee shop on Maple Street in 1978. "It was like an ice cream parlor. Instead of all the different flavors of ice cream there were all these different coffees. And the aroma." He remembers there were bins of medium and dark roasted beans. He took some coffee home. "And wow. This is so awesome I was blown away. It was fantastic. Better than anything I had ever drank." At the time, New Orleans coffee shops offered "a couple of coffees and coffee with chicory. What else do you want?" He spent the next six years working for PJ's.

Bob ticks off a few of the early coffeehouses in New Orleans serving specialty coffee: Coffee Chateau, True Brew, Plantation, Royal Blend and

Bob Arceneaux of Orleans Coffee. *Photo by David Feldman.*

A Rich History

Fair Grinds. "They were killing it," selling a lot of flavored coffees, single-origin coffees, espresso and blends. They "were foundational to specialty coffee. They were bringing coffee to the people." The equipment in those days was primitive in comparison with today: a Bunn coffee maker like you would see in any diner, a Bunn grinder and an espresso machine. Bob said, "For the time, the era, this is as good as anybody knew it was." And easy access to information was nonexistent. What took two years for Bob to learn through experience now takes minutes to find and bookmark on the internet.

Then Starbucks came in and reset the bar. Funky coffeehouses gave way to sleek, professionally designed ones. The coffee got more "specialty." The importers and coffee associations in the coffee growing regions began to organize trips. Bob recalled, "You got to know the farmer, his kids' names, his dog's name." Bob and his wife, on one trip, tasted over one hundred coffees in three days. "Talk about pallet [sic] fatigue." They kept raising the bar for the beans they imported, narrowing their focus from region down to farm to lot on that farm. "You reach a point where you gotta keep up with the Jones [sic]. You have to keep buying better coffee and better equipment."

Recent New Orleans history is divided in pre- and post-Katrina. Bob's roasting plant in the Gert Town section of New Orleans was flooded and destroyed in the hurricane. His eleven employees dispersed around the country, many never to be heard from again. He opened his current roastery and found himself educating and supplying coffee and equipment to the latest generation of New Orleans coffee bar *proprietários*.* Several of Bob's mentees now source and roast their own beans.

Bob was instrumental in educating and mentoring people who have gone on to owning their own coffee shops, sourcing their own beans and roasting their own profiles. All shop owners and staff who know Bob credit the vital support received from Orleans Coffee when they were just beginning. There is an irony in all of this. Bob explained, "Now, when coffeehouses roast their own beans, I become obsolete." But Orleans Coffee has two cafés, one uptown and one in the Zeitgeist Multi-Disciplinary Arts Center, in the American Sector, near the Dryades Market.

As for coffee at home, throughout the twentieth century, some New Orleanians were still brewing coffee the way their grandparents and great-grandparents had done. But others joined in drinking the main coffee sold

---

* Working on this book has caused me to consider that Hurricane Katrina in 2005 was a watershed moment for many New Orleanians and for coffee. Careers were interrupted. Many took refuge in coffeehouses. Others went to "temporary work" as baristas in those coffeehouses. A number of these people found a new passion and career in coffee. —David Feldman

in the United States. Some even drank instant coffee, although there appears to have always been a desire to improve on that experience. Home-brewing coffee concentrate was not unheard of. This was done generally by slowly pouring cold filtered water slowly over coffee grounds, at a ratio of eight to ten cups of water to one pound of coffee, letting the coffee sit for eight to twelve hours, then straining it.

CoolBrew

But one New Orleans family took this a step further. In 1986, Philip McCrory, who drank a lot of instant coffee, was given a Filtron cold water coffee brewer. This method of brewing cold coffee concentrate removes some of the oils and acidity from coffee. When Philip shared some of the coffee with his son Jeff and Jeff's friends, also instant coffee drinkers, Jeff said, "This is so good. We ought to put it in a bottle and sell it." His dad, who was director of pharmacy services in the Louisiana Office of Public Health, pulled out a pad of paper, and they began making plans. The operation started small, using two Dixie Beer kegs with the tops cut off and some retrofitted valves and a cotton filter made by the matriarch of the family, Colette, who was in the upholstery business. Thus CoolBrew, named by Philip McCrory, was born.

The first commercial office and factory was in a building Jeff's uncle owned in Covington, Louisiana, and the first accounts were New Orleans family-owned Dorignac's grocery store and a local Whole Foods outlet. Jeff recalled that "cold coffee was a hard sell. Not many people here drank instant coffee, and iced coffee was unheard of down here." At first, Jeff was working a day job and bottling and delivering the coffee at night. And the concept was new: people didn't know what to make of the unusual bottle, which has a one-ounce reservoir at the top that fills with the liquid when the bottle is squeezed. Now the bottle has a drawing to explain the instructions. This is still a family business, so Jeff's son Dylan's girlfriend Harli drew the picture.

The McCrory family first saw this bottle used for Delaware Punch (sold in the New Orleans drugstore chain K&B before it was sold in 1997). It also was in a packaging catalogue brought home by Phil. There was some concern that this bottle was commonly used for engine oil. As Jeff said, "Nobody's going to want to buy something edible out of that. It's hard enough selling cold coffee." But the bottle won over his objections. Both locals and many people were introduced to CoolBrew at the city's annual

A Rich History

Left: Philip McCrory, founder of CoolBrew; *Right*: Jeff McCrory, CEO of CoolBrew. *Photos by Suzanne Stone.*

JazzFest. Jeff and his brother noticed that people were reusing their bottles for alcohol. So, in 2019, specially labeled bottles were provided to the Muses Krewe as "throws" during the Muses Mardi Gras parade.

Roasting was first done at a small roasting company run by Roberto Gambini and Joe Marcello. Although repeatedly warned that the men might be connected with the mob (after all, the American Mafia started in New Orleans), Jeff pooh-poohed that idea. Then one night he learned that Gambini had been arrested for burning down a Miami coffee warehouse and fled New Orleans (and he was later convicted also of money laundering). The problem was that CoolBrew had nine hundred pounds of coffee in the Gambini warehouse. A friend had the key to the warehouse, so Jeff went in and salvaged the coffee. Only later did he learn from his brother, Greg, the company's CFO, that they had not yet paid for that coffee. Today, Dupuy's grinds and roasts the beans for CoolBrew. Jeff and others sample the coffee to ensure its quality and that the flavor matches their profile before buying it.

With persistence, the company—first known as Coffee Extractors of New Orleans—grew, winning more accounts and moving to a few facilities, each larger than the last, eventually setting up shop in Mid-City New Orleans. Beer kegs and homemade filters made way for mixing tanks from an old root beer plant and surplus equipment from the Luzianne instant coffee plant.

The McCrorys discovered they needed to explain how to use the CoolBrew bottle. *Image provided by CoolBrew.*

A Rich History

CoolBrew didn't turn a profit for almost twenty years, and then Katrina hit the city. With the factory and office under five feet of water, it took two years for CoolBrew to re-open, with a fleur-de-lis, the emblem of the city since Bourbon French days, on the label. Now known as New Orleans Coffee Company, CoolBrew makes about 150,000 gallons a year, and the brand is sold in about thirty states, through regional WalMart, Publix, Fresh Market and Whole Foods stores, as well as on Amazon and coolbrew.com. It was sold in California, but with the recent ruling requiring a label that says coffee causes cancer, Jeff, now the CEO of the company, won't sell there.

The New Orleans Coffee Company was concerned about the growth of the coffee grounds, which rose in proportion to the growth in the business. For the past ten years, the company has donated the grounds to EcoUrban, which transforms them into a premium composted garden soil for businesses and homes.

Coffee shops selling iced drinks—and their popularity in general—have fueled the growth of CoolBrew. CoolBrew started with coffee and chicory (what else in New Orleans?), a dark French Roast and various other flavors, in part to gain market share and in part to gain shelf space in groceries. Six flavors remain: in order of popularity, the coffee-chicory blend, mocha, vanilla, hazelnut, toasted almond and French Roast. Another boost to the company is its popularity with bartenders.

Plus, it is appreciated by many as their home coffee or for other drinks made at home. The commercially brewed concentrate is so popular that companies in at least seven other states, the District of Columbia and Japan have begun making similar products.

White Alligator
New Orleans Coffee Company's improvement on the White Russian

1 ounce Original CoolBrew Coffee Concentrate*
1 ounce vodka
3 ounces milk
Sugar or simple syrup, to taste

Mix all ingredients together. Shake or stir and serve over ice.

Note: Mocha, Vanilla, Hazelnut or Toasted Almond CoolBrew may be substituted in place of Original.

New Orleans Coffee

• • •

Midnight on the Bayou™
New Orleans Coffee Company's improvement to the Black Russian

1 ounce Original CoolBrew Coffee Concentrate
2 ounces vodka
1 ounce sugar or simple syrup

Mix all ingredients together. Shake or stir and serve over ice.

• • •

Ethel Stone's Coffee

My mother loved her coffee dark, strong and hot, but not too hot. For those instances when the coffee was too hot, and she did not have time to let it cool, she made coffee ice cube. These could be added to her drink without diluting it. If only she had known about home cold brewing or if CoolBrew had been marketed then, how much easier it would have been!

Arrow Coffee

Rampart Street was the old boundary of the original New Orleans, separating it from the plantation of Claude Tremé. It was named for the wooden wall that was built on the street in the city's early years as part of the city's fortifications. Now it traverses from the Central Business District to the Lower Ninth Ward. On the few blocks where it separates the French Quarter from the Tremé neighborhood are a number of places where New Orleanians have gathered for centuries. Just about halfway from Canal to Esplanade (the Quarter's boundaries) is Louis Armstrong Park, known before the Civil War as Congo Square. This was a place where enslaved

A Rich History

Sarah Cosiatto, co-owner of Arrow Coffee. *Photo by Suzanne Stone.*

people and free people of color gathered on Sundays. A building at the corner with Dumaine Street housed the J&M Recording Studio, where musical luminaries recorded. At the other end of the street stands Our Lady of Guadalupe Chapel, built in 1826 as the Mortuary Chapel to serve St. Louis Cemetery No. 1.

Now the street boasts Arrow Café, a new place for mixing and mingling. Owner Sarah Corsiatto greets almost every customer by name and can easily—if the press of business allows—catch up on the current news in their lives and share her updates. Sarah believes "coffee is a conversation starter." The shop also hosts monthly art shows as part of the mission to help artists start their careers. She and co-owner Nick Christian planned the shop as a bodega and wanted it to be a drop-in place for the neighborhood. Another part of the mission is to give back to the community. As Nick has said, "You can try to feed off the community, which is unfortunately what a lot of business do, or you can try to bring everyone together and give them a place to grow."

The entire operation has been "a labor of love" for both of them according to Sarah, who has been in the coffee business more than half her life, since she was fourteen. She and Nick first met in Portland. They met again in New Orleans, and when the opportunity arose to purchase Arrow in 2016, they decided to take the plunge. They both brought coffee shop experience to the venture. And they brought their vision and sense of mission.

Arrow Coffee sign. *Photo by Suzanne Stone.*

To meet their goals, they changed the entire interior to feature local artists and provide space for nonprofits' meetings and drop-in games. They also changed the food menu to appeal to both their usual customers and tourists. Most of all, there is ample space to sit and "schmooze." Sarah is aware of the power of conversations in coffee shops, stating that she "knows revolutions have started in coffee houses." The revolution their arrow points to is an appreciation of community.

Streetcar service, which ended in 1949, was reopened in 2016, leading to a growth in both tourists and locals traversing Rampart Street. Sarah knows that this only means increased business for Arrow. She and Nick are ready to welcome more people into the community established at Arrow Café. Sarah said that the business partnership she and Nick have forged "is the most functional relationship of her life." Their appreciation for each other and for good coffee, good conversations, good friends and doing something both fun and meaningful cements the relationship. It also cements their customer loyalty.

BACKATOWN: A COFFEE PARLOUR

One episode in New Orleans history seems to have no contributions to its coffee history: the twenty-year experiment with controlling sin, most specifically prostitution. In the late 1890s, city alderman Sidney Story oversaw establishment of an area in which prostitution, although still illegal,

A Rich History

was tolerated. Known officially as "the District," it soon was better known as "Storyville," named after the city alderman. The boundaries were North Robertson, Iberville, St. Louis and Basin Streets.* At 235 Basin Street was Mahogany Hall, the most lavish of the Jezebel Houses. Operated by Lulu White, the house contained five parlors decorated after exotic locales, an elevator for two and fifteen bedrooms well-mirrored with attached bathrooms on its four floors.

Mahogany Hall and the rest of Storyville are long gone, closed during World War I. The neighborhood, considered by many to be "Back of Town," as it was outside the original city's limits, has also undergone changes. The Iberville Projects replaced the fine homes run by the madams, or landladies, as they preferred to be called. And those have been torn down for further development. One of New Orleans' newest coffee shops, Backatown, is part of the redevelopment. It is on Basin Street, just steps away from what would have been number 235.

Owner Alonzo L. Knox, MBA, started Backatown after his partnership as co-owner of Café Tremé fell apart. An entrepreneur, Alonzo had been bitten by the coffee bug in that venture. Or at least with the "gathering place" bug common to many in coffee. Alonzo and his wife, Jessica, were active in the neighborhood association in Tremé and realized a spot was needed for neighbors to congregate. After it was established, that shop in the Tremé served many locals. When it closed, people came to Alonzo and Jessica, who also are business partners, asking for another shop to open up. They were eager to establish a place for "people, old and young, to do what they needed to do, socialize, study, hold business meetings." They found the space on Basin Street and discovered the owner was amenable to a coffee shop.

Jessica, the designing half of the duo, believed that the shop should provide some homage to the old neighborhood. The walls offer "a modern twist on Storyville." The art has an art deco feel that is right at home in a city that benefitted from many Depression-era works programs providing that style of art and architecture. The name, Backatown, came somewhat naturally and was tested in focus groups to ensure that it did not sound pejorative or suggestive. After all, New Orleans' "Back of Town," specifically Rampart Street, just one block away from Basin Street, was in 1910 "part of a bustling, diverse neighborhood that included grocery stores and restaurants, hotels [as well as] jazz-fueled honky tonks," according to Richard Campanella (quoted by James Karst).

---

* Basin Street gets its name because that was once the location of the turning basin of the Carondelet Canal.

Above: Backatown Coffee Parlour; *Right*: Alonzo Knox, co-owner of Backatown Coffee Parlour. *Photos by Suzanne Stone.*

So, while the coffee shop has nothing in common with the Storyville houses that used to line that block, it has much in common with the other neighborhood shops of yesteryear. As Alonzo said, "We strive to present Backatown as an authentic New Orleans gathering space that helps cultivate our neighborhoods through the fostering of ideas and conversations." Unlike other specialty coffee shops, Backatown is a parlor and includes comfy sofas and "light fare" meals along with the usual pastries. Not just Howard Schultz's "third place," Backatown's parlor atmosphere feels like home to Alonzo's former customers. Because of the location, just blocks from St. Louis Cemetery No. 1, tour companies have begun to use the location as a meeting spot or break location. More and more tourists are discovering that they can find the comforts of home here, too.

Cherry Coffee

By David Feldman

Lauren Fink of Cherry Coffee Roasters remembers her "aha" coffee moment. The first time she smelled "naturally dried in the fruit coffee" she pulled up, "Whoa! I smell berries." Lauren grew up in a small town in Wisconsin. She copped to drinking iced caramel lattes as a teenager when she and her mom hit the Starbucks drive-through. Lauren's progression from iced caramel lattes to lattes to macchiatos seems natural and logical, in retrospect. Ultimately, only espresso and pour-over coffee were left. The milk and sugar were gone. But, as she explained, "You really taste the unique characteristics of the individual coffee."

Unraveling, Lauren's word, the marvelous complexity of coffee for herself is her passion. Sharing what she has learned with her customers and employees at her two coffee shops is both a passion and a mission. She dreams of a time when "the normal thing for people to drink is black coffee," along with other coffee drinks. Lauren's coffee journey began in a coffee shop next to the college in her small hometown. The coffee probably wasn't specialty, but they did roast their own. The fresher the roasting, grinding and brewing, the more likely the coffee will taste and smell better. Lauren fondly remembers the tips the students left.

Portland, a West Coast coffee mecca, beckoned. "I was a farmer and a barista. I grew hydroponic tomatoes." She also learned to "pull a shot" of

Lauren Fink, owner, Cherry Coffee. *Photo by David Feldman.*

espresso. Pulling a great but never perfect shot of espresso, "dialing it in," as Lauren puts it, is the mark of an accomplished professional barista. The characteristics of the roasted coffee, the fineness of the grind, the weight of the coffee, the temperature of the water, the pressure forcing the water through the grind, the length of extraction time are to name but a few of the variables.

Lauren needed the sun, though. "I packed up the pickup and the dog and headed south." She stopped to work in Austin briefly before coming to New Orleans to stay in 2011. She worked as a barista at several local coffee shops for a couple of years. "I had never thought once that I would own a coffee shop," Lauren admitted. Her passion for everything coffee, though, was especially apparent to one person, her dad. "My Dad was like 'why don't you try to do your own thing?'" Lauren began to consider what she wanted to do with her life. Did she want to go back to school? She decided, "I really wanted to be in coffee." Her dad helped her get a loan, and she bought an espresso machine. In June 2013, she opened as a pop-up coffee shop in the very popular Stein's Deli on Magazine Street. Lauren worked every day for a year making the pop-up successful with a loyal following. She "dreamed of getting out of the deli."

Lauren secured a bank loan and an SBA loan, and the first Cherry Coffee opened in 2016 in Uptown New Orleans, two years after signing the papers. "What's in a name?" Lauren hopes you'll ask. The fruit of the coffee tree that contains the coffee bean or seed is called a cherry. It's cranberry shaped and bright red when ripe.

One of the first things Lauren learned was that there were not enough professional baristas to go around in New Orleans. She resolved to train her own. "We do things a certain way here," so she prefers to train people without coffee experience. Lauren travels a lot, to Chicago, Portland, Seattle. She believes that her baristas serve some of the best coffee anywhere, not just New Orleans. "That speaks volumes of the training process," she said.

A second and very important lesson learned was that for her customers to be open to the full experience of specialty coffee, she had to make it less unapproachable, alienating, fearful. Toward that end, her baristas are not only welcoming but encouraged to offer new taste experiences. Lauren

Cherry Coffee. *Photo by David Feldman.*

conducts palate development tastings. Foods are sampled with special attention paid to how they taste. Discussion follows. Then a cup of coffee is served, and the same processes are applied. The idea is to make coffee more accessible by developing the vocabulary to talk about it.

Only a year after opening the first shop, Lauren raised $25,000 in a Kickstarter campaign. She opened a second shop and a coffee roastery. Cherry Coffee became Cherry Coffee Roaster. Lauren explained, "Roasting my own beans was the natural next step" in broadening and deepening her knowledge of coffee. The roastery opened in the basement of a public school converted to artists' studios and craft workshops in the Katrina-devastated Lower Ninth Ward. Six months after firing up, the roastery is supplying half the coffee to the Uptown shop and all the coffee to the Magazine Street store.

Lauren Fink is "dialing in" her roasting just as she and her baristas dial in the espresso shots every morning—trial and error and taste.

Coast Roast

The next chapter in New Orleans coffee history is that the twenty-first century is seeing a rebirth of some of the neighborhood markets. The Dryades Market, established in 1849, is the new home of the Southern Food and Beverage Museum, which includes the Leah Chase Louisiana Gallery.* The museum also contains a wide variety of artifacts from the region's coffee history. St. Roch Market, originally an open-air market on the corner of St. Claude and St. Roch Avenues, thrived from its beginning in 1875 into bare survival by the end of the Great Depression. St. Roch was a privately owned seafood market in the late twentieth century before Katrina severely damaged both the interior and exterior of the building. St. Roch Market has reopened as a neighborhood market complete with one dozen vendors selling breakfast, lunch, snacks and handmade grocery items. It also includes a coffee shop.

Kevin Pedeaux and his partner, Shawn Montella, roast on two antique Royal #6 seventy-pound roasters that they have taken apart and rebuilt "about 1,000 times." The partners met in Long Beach, Mississippi, where Kevin's great-grandfather built a summer home, which is now around the corner from Shawn's coffee shop. Kevin was working for Randazzo Bakery, serving the PJ's account. Every time he made a delivery to one PJ's, "someone would say, 'hey Kevin, want a cup of coffee?' And then I'd go to the next PJ's and someone would say 'Hey, do you want a cup of coffee?'" He drank an African coffee at one stop and a Mexican coffee at another and started learning about coffee. This led to conversations with Shawn and eventually the partnership.

The first account was Randazzo, when Kevin showed the owner what coffee he had obtained from Shawn. Next came Coffee Rani, with shops in Mandeville and Covington, across Lake Pontchartrain from New Orleans. Kevin tried to sell to a farmer's market in Covington and learned that local Coffee Rani sponsored the market, so he pitched to the owner, who "came on board. With two accounts, I decided to jump in the coffee business," said Kevin. That was June 2009. His goal is to make and sell coffee "that tastes like coffee, only better."

Kevin learned about roasting from Bruce Walle, a longtime Westfeldt employee and the connection from Westfeldt's to Shawn. Kevin acknowledged, "Bruce forgot more about roasting than I'll ever know." He learned the old-school methods from Bruce: "what coffee should smell like,

---

* A new Dryades Public Market has opened a few blocks away in a converted school.

Roaster that is used at Coast Roast. *Courtesy of Kevin Pedeaux.*

what it should look like." Bruce was ill with a fatal brain cancer toward the end of the lessons, and Kevin remembered one time when "I served him some coffee, and Bruce signaled for a napkin and pencil since it was difficult for him to talk, and then he drew the profile of the coffee I'd served him. Next he drew a big X over my mistake and showed the correction that was needed. I've never made that mistake again."

Kevin Pedeaux, co-owner of Coast Roast Coffee. *Photo by Suzanne Stone.*

Kevin believes "coffee is a fun business to be in." Coast Roast is primarily a roasting company for some of the many coffee shops in New Orleans. Kevin maintained, "The most satisfying part of my business is helping a new business grow and become successful. It's very rewarding to see the coffee business grow." One of his newest accounts is Café au Play, built with families and kids in mind. He found this account in a typical New Orleans way: through individual contacts. The woman who makes Coast Roast's signage had begun to design Café au Play's logo and put Kevin in touch with the owners, Kara and James Hayes. After talking with a number of suppliers and tasting their coffee, they went with Coast Roast. They seem to agree with Kevin and Shawn that the coffee is what people come for, and wanting all ages to feel welcome, they've designed a child-appropriate drink, warm milk in a coffee cup topped with sprinkles, called the Charlieccino after their daughter.

While Kevin and Shawn never planned on a coffee shop, the spot at St. Roch called to them; among a dozen food vendors, the Coast Roast shop focuses solely on coffee. And conversation. "This is a public market; it's a cool space for people to hang out. It's a place where people meet, just to be social." Kevin thinks that coffee serves as "the blank canvas for conversation." And like the coffee shops of old, there is a wide variety of conversations at Coast Roast. Kevin hosts "Coffee with Kevin" on YouTube, which consist of recordings of various conversations at the shop. Some of these are about coffee, some about life and some about politics. In the last local election cycle, Kevin invited in all the mayoral candidates for conversation. "The real rewarding part of the job is my relationships, with those who come in the shop, with my wholesale customers. Over the years, we've become friends. People are the important part."

A Rich History

Congregation Coffee

By David Feldman

Eliot Guthrie was working in restaurants and food service in Seattle and wanted to relocate to New Orleans. Ian Barrilleaux, Louisiana born and bred, was a butcher and charcutier curing meats and game at Cochon, a popular restaurant in New Orleans. Ian hired Eliot. Eliot had been exposed to very good coffee in Seattle. As he said, "It's not hard to be." He saw a void in the market. Restaurants with great food weren't serving great coffee. "We both saw there was an opportunity," Eliot explained. They bought a small roaster and began to experiment with beans and roasting about six hours a week in Eliot's Mid-City shed. "We found some beans that we liked, a profile we liked and shopped it around to a few restaurants." They were in business. Multiple surveys among friends and family resulted in the name, Congregation.

Three years later, 2018, Congregation has some of New Orleans' best restaurants as wholesale customers, a mail-order business and a roastery and coffee bar in the Algiers neighborhood across the river from the French Quarter. Congregation occupies a wide-open, high-ceilinged nineteenth-century wooden structure. Eliot's dad came east to help with the build out. Congregation is now one big room about forty by eighty feet under a fourteen-foot ceiling, clear space save for two rows of columns. A coffee fairy dropped a Marzocco espresso machine and grinder on their doorstep. The coffee bar is front and center. Neighbors pop in and out all day. Hearty "coffee" tourists take the ferry over to sample their coffee. Just behind the bar is the eighteen-pound coffee roaster, the heart of the business. Bags of green coffee are stored on pallets around the building.

Eliot and Ian have a laser-like focus on their business: to improve the coffee in New Orleans' restaurants and coffee bars. Eliot remembered, "We knew going in we were going to have to change restaurants' willingness to spend more money on coffee. That was a hard enough sale." Their pitch is: "This will be a better cup of coffee. You will get compliments on it. People are going to enjoy it more and more." They supply the coffee, equipment and service to make that happen once they acquire an account.

Congregation Coffee concentrates on only a few blended and roasted coffees. This limited repertoire allows them maximum control over the quality, consistency and freshness their customers demand. This task is not as easy as it sounds. "In coffee we have the Rule of Fifteen....Green coffee beans should be roasted within 15 months of harvest; ground and brewed within 15 days of roasting and served and drunk within 15 minutes to be at its flavorful best."

Roasting is as much art as science. Somewhere in pre-recorded history, humankind discovered that if you cooked your food and boiled your beverages they smelled better, tasted better and were more easily digested. In the early twentieth century a French chemist, Maillard, described what came to be known as the Maillard reaction. As you apply heat, in this case to green coffee beans, the amino acids and residual sugars combine to create new molecules, which give rise to new aromas and flavors. The amount of heat applied, the rate of temperature "rise" and the length of time in the roaster are some of the variables.

The computer hooked to Congregation's Pilot roaster profiles what is happening in the drum. Ultimately, though, it comes down to someone's senses of smell, taste and touch. That someone at Congregation is Sarah Lambeth. She has a long history in coffee, beginning as a barista. Sarah competes successfully in the Specialty Coffee Association national cup tasting competitions. Eighteen cups of coffee are divided into six

Using the Prabat Roaster at Congregation Coffee. *Photo by David Feldman.*

A Rich History

Sarah Lambeth (*left*), Ian Barrilleaux (*middle*) and Eliot Guthrie (*right*) at Congregation Coffee. *Photo by David Feldman.*

groups of three. One in each group of three is slightly different. The winner must find it faster than anyone else. Sarah is the educated palate of Congregation, and she spends a day and a half to two days a week roasting and sampling coffees.

Eliot and Ian are very much aware of the long history of New Orleans coffee. As Eliot put it, "The tradition can be rewritten while being honored." Dark, almost burned, French Roast coffee and coffee with chicory "hold a special place" in New Orleans' lore and love of coffee. Congregation now offers a rendition of both.

Eliot avowed, "If we got the opportunity to open a counter in the French Quarter and serve beignets I probably wouldn't say no." But, he emphasized, "It would be our coffee and our take on beignets."

Fair Grinds

By David Feldman

Wade Rathke bought Fair Grinds Coffee from Robert and Elizabeth Thompson in 2011. Longtime patrons and neighbors of the Faubourg Saint John gathering place made it clear that he was under probation. "They were very skeptical when we took over," Wade said. A group of regulars had been meeting most mornings for more than a dozen years to talk politics and gossip around the big center table. People "were afraid we might put a coat of paint on the walls."

After all, the late nineteenth-century building just a block from Fair Grounds race track had a rich and varied history. While renovating in the early 2000s, Robert Thompson uncovered two painted murals; one of the finish line at the Fair Grounds Race Track and a second of a horse in the winner's circle at the track. Upstairs, Thompson found six phone lines in the walls.

Chaco (*left*) and Wade Rathke, proprietors of the only Fair Trade coffee in New Orleans. *Photo by Suzanne Stone.*

It was a bookmaking parlor. Through the years, the building has housed an Italian grocery, coffeehouses and numerous bars.

"We've heard a thousand rumors about this place, all real sordid," remembered Elizabeth Thompson. A country girl came to town to work in the French Quarter. She found a sugar daddy to buy the place for her. A horse trainer made a killing at the track that he tried to hide from his lover. She found out, came to the bar and shot him. Another fellow was beaten to death with pool cues then dragged to the house next door.

Being near the race track—home to the city's annual Jazz Fest—still affects Fair Grinds. Those three spring weekends are the busiest time of the year for the store. Manager Chaco Rathke remembered one time as the fest was closing for the day, "a wasted customer came in and asked if we sell beer. I said no, but that I could provide a special cup of coffee for $3.00. He paid $10.00 for the cup and went away. The next evening he returned with his friend and paid $10.00 again for a $3.00 cup of coffee."

A Rich History

The three recent incarnations as a coffeehouse have secured the building's place in New Orleans' coffee life and lore. In the late 1970s and early 1980s, Pat and Denise Winegarter opened True Brew Coffee House there. They were among the pioneers in New Orleans serving specialty coffee. The Winegarters made the upstairs space available for a full calendar of events: poetry readings, musical performances, art shows and community meetings. The Thompsons carried on this tradition under the name Fair Grinds. In fact, Wade said, "the social and political values" of Fair Grinds through the decades were a large part of the reason he bought it.

Wade kept the name and values and added the slogan, "Great Coffee for a Change." It is a very appropriate play on words. For almost half a century Wade Rathke has not only been talking the talk but also walking the walk of community organizing for social justice and change in the United States and around the world. An organization he founded in the 1970s is credited with some of the nation's first living wage laws, registering more than a million voters and promoting fair housing laws.

Fair Grinds menu. *Photo by Suzanne Stone.*

Fair Grinds' mission, according to Wade, "is to serve our local community by providing delicious coffee, a full cafe menu, and space for neighbors to meet and exchange ideas." That mission has ripple effects far beyond the shop. Fair Grinds is New Orleans' only 100 percent Fair Trade (FT) coffeehouse. Wade explained, "Part of our overall mission and politics is that people get paid a living wage." More than twenty million people around the world depend on the coffee chain for their living from the growers to the barista artistically decorating your latte. To be certified Fair Trade, organic coffee is grown in producer-owned cooperatives. A producer might be a woman working a quarter acre in northern India. Child and forced labor are prohibited. The growers and the co-ops must use sustainable agricultural and environmentally friendly processing practices. The coffee is produced to the highest standards. In return, the producers receive a premium per pound over the price of coffee on the commodity exchange.

It is an expensive proposition for Fair Grinds. "Others get coffee at half the price we pay." Yet, as Wade explained, "We have to sell it for the same price as PJ's or Starbucks." Sometimes his cost of coffee beans is 80–90 percent higher. Doing the right thing does not come cheaply.

Wade has taken this mission several steps further. He incorporated Fair Grinds as a low-profit social venture. He sends 5 percent of his gross to the cooperatives in the producing countries. "On a half million gross that's about $20,000 to $25,000 a year." Closer to home, Wade insists that his coffee be shipped to the Port of New Orleans and handled on the docks by union workers. Much of the produce on his café menu comes from a garden Fair Grinds volunteers cultivate in the Lower Ninth Ward. There is a full monthly calendar of events in the upstairs community space, used by nonprofits and twelve-step programs.

Wade came off of probation in August 2012. Hurricane Isaac swept through New Orleans, and 80 percent of the city was without power. Fair Grinds had a generator. It stayed open, the lights and the aroma of brewing coffee beckoning. After the hurricane had passed, Wade remembered, "I came in and all of a sudden the big table and everyone else stood up and was clapping. We were okay after that."

By the way, Fair Grinds may be the only coffeehouse in the world where you can get an organic, Fair Trade coffee with chicory. Only in New Orleans.

French Truck

More than just IT firms start in family garages, basements and kitchens. In 2012, Geoffrey Meeker received a bag of freshly roasted coffee from a cousin and was amazed at the difference in taste compared with his usual coffee. He began roasting fresh coffee in a ten-pound roaster in his laundry room. A friend, Bobby Winston, was doing the same in his kitchen and kept nagging Geoffrey to join forces together.

Within a year, Geoffrey had expanded to a thirty-pound roaster and was ready for a partner. Expansion called for innovation: moving out of the laundry and kitchen, but not into a larger, commercial kitchen like everyone else, but into a French truck. Geoffrey bought a Citroen 2CV (*deux chevaux* in French), a two-horsepower, air-cooled, front-engine, front-wheel-drive car to serve as both the roaster and delivery van. Thus, French Truck coffee expanded into both home delivery and pop-up appearances at the Palmer Park Arts Market, held on the last Saturday of every month at the corner where South Carrollton and South Claiborne Streets intersect (only in New Orleans, where most streets follow the bends of the Mississippi River rather than cardinal directions).

Bobby said, "Like a puppy, the Citroen 2CV quickly brings a smile to one's face…and now reminds everyone in New Orleans of a particular coffee brand," served in over fifty restaurants and at six locations (and growing), as well as sold in twelve-ounce packages (meant to be used in one week) in groceries. One of the objectives, he said, "is to change people's perceptions of coffee's freshness." All coffee is stored no more than six months and roasted in-house within two weeks of arrival.

In addition to using the freshest ingredients possible and serving them as soon as possible after production—the antithesis of mass production—Geoffrey and Bobby are guided by a desire to import the best beans from a variety of sources. Bobby, now the Green Buyer and QC Manager, remembers his first taste of Ethiopian coffee in a shop in Colorado. "I tasted something new: blackberry and floral notes and fell into the 'rabbit hole' of coffee learning, lore, and love." French Truck began importing coffees from small farms via an offer list from their importers, but the partners soon realized they wanted and needed to know more about the coffee. So they now travel to the countries from which they import coffee, including Peru, Mexico, Guatemala, Kenya, Nicaragua, Ethiopia and Sumatra and get to know the farmers. They've learned that "some of the best coffee is not even making it on the offer list," according to Bobby. "You have to get first in line to get that stuff." These trips can get a bit manic, what with tasting fifty to one hundred coffees in three days. After acquisition, Geoffrey and Bobby develop the roasting profiles, changing with the season and carefully controlled with computer programs. Included in their offerings is a coffee chicory mix.

Taken with the stories of these farmers, French Truck includes a blurb about the farm from which the coffee comes on every package. For example, one farm is Kossa Geshe in Ethiopia. One reason for the high quality is the natural spring on the farm that provides an organic source of water. Geoffrey and Bobby also point out how increased sales have benefitted the communities: in Kossa Geshe, Bobby explained, "the owners now provide a nursery and elementary school, which has benefited the 25–50 year-round workers and their children, because previously the nearest school was 25 miles away."

Above: Cole Bonner (*left*) and Bobby Winston of French Truck Coffee. *Photo by David Feldman.*

Right: The Citroen 2CV in which French Truck Coffee started. *Image from website.*

A Rich History

French Truck owners are big believers in education and training, not just for themselves, but their staff. All baristas get a basic Coffee 101, based on the programs from the Specialty Coffee Association. Baristas, in turn, educate customers. Only never before that first cup in the morning! Others learn roastery techniques. Geoffrey and Bobby also believe in rewarding employees as their company grows and have recently added health insurance benefits.

Their growth is due, Bobby believes, to the quality of the coffee and the quality of their service.

Hey! Café

It is really possible to make lemonade out of lemons or a thriving coffee business out of a recession. Just ask Tommy LeBlanc, or Tommy L as he is known, co-owner of Hey Coffee Company and Hey! Coffee Cafés. Educated as an artist, Tommy had an animation business, making animated cartoon films for a former child star. Though small (recording in his high-ceilinged bedroom closet), it was thrumming along until 2008, when, as he says, "the money dried up." He was a caricature artist at the Riverwalk by the Mississippi, continuing this on weekends, including the Saturday in 2005 when Katrina evacuation from New Orleans became mandatory. This was annoying because he had "a long line of customers who now dispersed."

Tommy went to work at Magazine Perks, a coffee shop on Magazine Street, and got to know both the owner—who had mistakenly thought running a coffee shop was a great retirement occupation—and fellow employee Greg Rodrigue. Tommy was familiar with the shop because right out of college, he had taken a seasonal job at a costume shop a few doors down and enjoyed his coffee breaks at Magazine Perks. He liked it: "It was very approachable and appreciated by the customers, who checked in every day. Many of us felt it was our families' main hub."

When the owner realized moving to Mexico would be a better retirement option, Tommy and Gregory took over the shop's lease and changed the name to Hey! Café. They cleaned up the place, using Tommy's art to decorate and as their logo. Immediately, they both wanted to improve the coffee that had been served and, as novices, switched roasters and started learning about coffee. Immediately, the café's customers, already grateful they had kept the place open, complimented them on the improved brew.

Tommy LeBlanc with his roaster. *Photo by David Feldman.*

The next step was learning how to roast, which they did with a "toaster roaster," as Tommy calls it, a small roaster about the size of a toaster. Able to roast only half a pound at a time, Tommy used his shed for his "nano roasting," making enough to keep one carafe filled at all times in the store. Using this roaster was a learning experience, and Tommy continued learning online and from colleagues like Orleans Coffee's Bob Arceneaux. By 2014, he was ready to move up to a two-kilo roaster.

By then, he was "obsessed with coffee, getting the best available and learning how to bring out the flavor by roasting." Wholesale accounts started coming in, and Hey Coffee Company opened its own roasting facility, with a small Hey! Café up front. This new facility overlooks the Lafitte Greenway, a pedestrian and bicycle path running from the Lakeview neighborhood through Tremé, Lafitte and Mid-City neighborhoods into the outskirts of the French Quarter. Tommy enjoys looking out into the greenery, which includes landscape elements designed to remove pollution out of surface runoff and waste.

The company and cafés are committed to transparency in the coffee business, buying only from fair trade farms, and committed to recycling. Tommy explained, "We use pasta noodles for straws and cups that are biodegradable." Their efforts are successful, resulting in less than three pounds of trash daily. In examining places to buy their coffee, Tommy and Gregory have learned, "the more we look, the more we find people doing inspiring things." One example is the Guatemalan farm from which they get their coffee. A son of the farm's owner has moved to the area, joined the roasting business in the city and brings back to his village educational materials.

Tommy chose the name Hey! Café because "coffee is a conversation starter, a good way to say "hey!"" Also, it allowed him to make a coffee cup with a mouth on it, something his artistic instinct was itching to do.

Prizing hospitality as a watchword of the business, Tommy and Gregory make sure that among the food offered, there will be something for people who cannot eat certain foods, for health, religious, or other reasons. In

Hey Coffee Shop. *Photo by David Feldman.*

addition to constantly learning and improving the coffee and the hallmark hospitality, Tommy attributes their success to persistence, a trait recognized and appreciated by all New Orleanians.

Mojo

Demian Estevez is a New Orleanian through and through. He was conceived and raised in his early years in an apartment above legendary Johnny White's Bar in the French Quarter, which didn't close its doors during Hurricane Katrina and the terrible aftermath. Demian ventured outside his home city for only a few months after Katrina, and returned from road trips exploring potential new cities to move to with two realizations: "I can't live anywhere else, and I love coffee." He had a brief thought about staying in Terre Haute when he saw in that city surrounded by universities, colleges, and institutes a coffee shop with a sign, "No students allowed."

Fortuitously, those leasing space at his New Orleans neighborhood coffee shop, Café rue de la Course, decided to move on, and Demian and his wife, Angie, rented the space. They cleaned up the damage from the hurricane's winds and local looters and decorated in a funky New Orleans style, with tables and a bar Demian and his uncle built. The lease started in November 2005, just a little over two months after Katrina devasted the city, and they opened in March 2006. Given the difficulties in doing just about anything in this city then, they scrounged for equipment on eBay and elsewhere and even used triple-bagged paint strainers as coffee strainers.

Demian grew up with his Guatemalan father and mother from Texas drinking mass-marketed brew, including instant, and not realizing there was anything else. In his twenties, he discovered some of the first Third Wave coffee in New Orleans: Gloria Jean's (no longer in Louisiana), PJ's and the now-defunct but fabled Kaldi's. It was at Kaldi's, near the French Market, that Demian first realized that baristas were something vastly different from servers. The coffee was good, hot and strong. The customers were diverse: students, tourists, homeless, young people starting out and an older working crowd. Demian said simply, "I found home." But he kept his day job in computer networking.

His road trip after Katrina encouraged Demian to learn more about coffee, which led to his shop. He and his wife, Angie, started small, purchasing roasted coffee from their importers and local coffee roasters. But Demian continued his love affair with coffee, joining the Specialty Coffee Association and the Barista Guild Association, learning from his peers and taking first Barista Boot Camp I and then the second camp. These classes made him realize that the world of coffee was large, diverse and ever-changing; what he knew was passé and what he did not know was fascinating. He began buying coffee from more places and hired a roasting manager. The shop

A Rich History

Left: Mojo Café; *Below*: Mojo Café interior.
Photos by Suzanne Stone.

now has a modern roaster, connected to a computer with their coffee profiles programmed in. And he's passionate about education for his baristas and other staff. His baristas are members of the local Barista Social Club and regularly participate in—and win—latte throw downs.

Demian is proud that the shop buys only highly graded coffee and that their roasting improves the original score, by as much as eight points. He is also pleased that the ambience at Mojo's is focused on only two things: the coffee and the people. Mojo also typified the neighborhood hangout. When it first replaced Café de la Chase, some longtime customers did not know what to make of the interloper, but they all have been won over. Already a favorite place for locals, in 2008, Mojo cemented its love affair with the community. Having generators to stay open and brew coffee when Hurricane Gustav hit, Mojo's was one of the few places people could go to escape the driving rains. Staff helped neighbors board up homes, and they were helped in return. When the shop ran out of milk, a customer sought out a nearby mart at a gas station and brought back the necessary latte ingredient. Demian remembers that with most of the electricity out on Magazine Street and surrounding areas, he walked out and saw the "mojo sign glowing on the dark street," like a welcoming lighthouse beacon to ships at sea.

Demian Estevez, like the plot in the Herman Hesse novel for which he is named, struggled between two worlds—the corporate IT one and the coffee one. His struggle is over; he is at home fully in the world of coffee.

SPITFIRE

Byron Gomez followed his heart's desire—a career in music—to Nashville, where he fell down the "rabbit hole of coffee" and has emerged as the manager of perhaps the country's smallest coffee shop.

Spitfire Coffee is so small that it is described as being in a closet and can easily be missed by the casual stroller on St. Peter Street. It is sandwiched in between Skull Paradise and Pipe Dreams boutiques and directly across the street from the building where Tennessee Williams lived when he wrote *A Streetcar Named Desire*. But those who walk on by are missing the coffee shop in New Orleans most appreciated by foreign guests. Byron estimates that 60 percent of the customers are from Europe, Canada, South and Central America and Australia. "The business just snowballed. Some is word of mouth, some repeat customers, and then there are the airline magazines that mention us." Wherever they hear of Spitfire, customers from outside the United States constantly tell Byron and his baristas that "this is an oasis from the insanity of the French Quarter. Thank you so much; I haven't had a good cup of coffee in weeks." And business among locals is picking up. Byron enjoys serving "others in the service industry and the street musicians" who work within steps from Spitfire.

The coffee shop was named by its first owner, cinematographer John Peters; the story goes, his father flew the legendary plane during World War II. Now owned by Scott Burlington, the shop remains in its "closet," which has also served as an art studio.

The pour-over coffee and espressos come from a variety of roasters, including one of the newest in New Orleans: Exile Coffee Roasters. Named because Byron is a "Cajun (Acadian) boy exiled from the homeland," it is currently run out of Byron's kitchen and is capable of producing only a few five-pound bags of coffee each day. But expanding this side of his business will be the culmination of Byron's rabbit hole venture. "From day one, I wanted to buy, roast, and completely be part of the system that can impact from seed to cup." That day was as a part-time employee in a Nashville coffee shop, taken because his music gigs had dried up. He started out not even being a coffee drinker, but within a week, both he and his boss felt he had a future in coffee. His "Coffee 101" training taught him about the industry "from seed to cup" and convinced him that what he thought was "a $3.00 vice could have a positive global impact." This shop was buying from small farms and trying to give back to them. That "fueled the fire" for a Louisiana boy who wanted to make a difference in the world.

Moving to New Orleans in 2012, Byron noticed a surprising lack of specialty coffee shops. He worked at a local PJ's and at Café Tremé before getting the opportunity to join Spitfire in September 2013, just a few months after it opened. He noticed that the city—known for culinary advancement—was somewhat surprisingly hidebound when it came to coffee. While there were specialty coffee shops in the city, there "was not a community around specialty coffee as has developed since 2012." Byron said that has developed and "he loves being part of it."

Byron also believes that the definition of specialty coffee maybe should go beyond the current one based on grade to include the treatment of the bean and recognition of the volatility of the product. "We now are diving deep and tracing our dollar back to the very hands that grew the beans, picked and sorted them, and roasted them. All of these aspects should be referred to in terming something specialty coffee." Also, Byron is adamant

Above: Customer at Spitfire Coffee;
Right: Byron Gomez at Spitfire Coffee.
Photos by Suzanne Stone.

that "we should not be afraid of diversity in coffee." "It is the most diverse product under the sun, so attempts to make every cup taste the same don't make sense. Here at Spitfire, we go through so many different coffees and we're really trying to embrace that insanity that everything is unique and every cup has a story to tell." His new heart's desire is to be part of the "next chapter of New Orleans coffee."

Solo Espresso Bar

By David Feldman

Lauren Morlock and her husband bought a building about as far downriver in the Bywater neighborhood as you can go without falling into the Industrial Canal. It was August 2012. The building had been abandoned since Katrina in 2005. The windows and doors were boarded up. There was no electricity or water. Lauren remembered, "We closed on it the day [Hurricane] Isaac hit." Isaac left a three-foot high-water mark on the ground-floor wainscoting. They moved in anyway. "It was fun. Nobody had electricity," she recalled. They ran extension cords from neighbors and showered and charged their power tool batteries at their local gym. But the building, with living space upstairs and almost a thousand feet of unfinished space on the ground floor, was perfect for what she had in mind.

After working in a couple of New Orleans coffeehouses, Lauren decided she wanted to do her own thing in coffee. She had $10,000 and a lot of experience. As a teenager, she hung around in the coffee shop her mother managed in Bradenton, Florida. When she was old enough, she got a job as a barista there. After a stint with the same company in Tampa, Lauren moved to Miami to go to college for fashion design. She put herself through college working at Starbucks.

In those days, Starbucks had a training program called the Coffee Passport. "It was still a very hands-on company," Lauren explained. In meetings, baristas learned about the origins of the coffees they served. They had cuppings where they learned to identify the flavor profiles of the different coffees. "We wrote everything down in the Passport," she related. Lauren stayed with Starbucks and became a shift manager before moving to Seattle, a mecca of specialty coffee. In Seattle, working at Café Vita and All City Coffee, she learned roasting techniques, proper extraction and latte art. She values latte art because "it shows that the

Above: Solo Café owner Lauren Morlock (*far left*); *Left*: Solo's espresso machine. *Photos by David Feldman.*

barista knows how to properly extract espresso, pull a proper shot and steam and aerate the milk."

Lauren's first New Orleans opportunity was supposed to be a mobile coffee pop-up at a local Bywater bar. She knew that when she started her own business she "would want a Synesso Cyncra first generation espresso machine." The Synessos are hand-built in Seattle. She speaks of the gleaming stainless machine on her counter as a concert violinist might speak of her Stradivarius. "This is the machine I worked on in Seattle," said

A Rich History

Lauren. "It is a beautiful work horse....If you know how to use them, they make delicious coffee and last forever." She found a used one in Lafayette, Lousiana, and $8,500 later, she brought her beloved Synesso home and put it in the unfinished ground floor. "I knew what was important," she said laughingly. The coffee pop-up never materialized.

But Lauren did have an espresso machine, a mascot, her dog Shinobi and a name she had picked up in Peru: Solo, short for the Spanish *solomente*. As Lauren explained, after her years in coffee she resolved that "If I ever open a coffee shop it will be just coffee. No blended drinks, no frou frou this, no frou frou that." Solomente means "only." Only coffee. Good coffee, because as Lauren says, "I am part of a chain that extends from the farmer to the roaster to the barista, and each person in that chain has to follow best practices, in growing, shipping, storing, roasting, and then serving." Her employees share this philosophy. Theodore Lloyd-Hughes, the barista with the longest tenure, was interviewing for a job when Lauren noticed the portafilter tattooed on his forearm. "I hired him right away. Never been sorry." (A portafilter is the part of an espresso machine that holds the coffee.)

She "opened" in June 2013 as the Solo Espresso Bar/Speakeasy. The "opened" is in quotes because there actually was no there, there, only an espresso machine in an unfinished, unlicensed space. Lauren distributed flyers throughout the neighborhood asking people to call to order. And they did. Her customers would knock on the door to pick up their coffee, or she would deliver by bicycle or car. Lauren's stepdad came to help with the buildout of the first four hundred square feet. Just as Solo was outgrowing that space, some local carpenters became regulars at the shop and, as Lauren remembers, "they told me that they would help with our build out, providing work and furniture in trade for coffee."

Lauren buys from a Miami roaster, Panther Coffee. Solo serves Panther's East Coast Espresso blend, a "very, very palatable drink." She had noticed that "coffee in New Orleans was dark and bitter" compared to what she knew and liked. "I wanted to lighten up the coffee scene, but some people thought a lighter roast was sour. So I ended up with a more nuanced flavor; the cherries and chocolate" in the East Coast Espresso seems to please just about everyone.

There is one concession Lauren will not make. "My shop has no wifi—and never will." For Lauren, "It's all about relationships." She relishes the relationships she has with her employees, her customers and the relationships that flower at the long, communal table in the back of Solo. The quietly soothing space has several cozy conversation nooks. The image in the logo is

Lauren's dog, Shinobi, who has since passed on. He was her only companion all day, every day in the beginning. "Sometimes we didn't sell 10 coffees a day." Lauren explained, "I didn't open a coffee shop to make money. I like seeing everyone here, talking with one another, making friends and forming relationships."

New Orleans' Coffee Women

New Orleans boasts three women in the coffee business, in addition to many coffee shop owners and baristas.

Phyllis Jordan was a social worker before exploring her entrepreneurial side. After relocating from Iowa to New Orleans, she opened the first PJ's Coffee & Tea Company in the city's Carrollton neighborhood. This was in 1978, and hers was one of the first specialty coffee shops outside the West Coast. Her own personality—optimistic and joyful—played a part in her wanting to be involved in a social business. She encountered many obstacles—being new to the city, having little funding and being a woman.

Phyllis Jordan, founder of PJ's Coffee and former president, Specialty Coffee Association of America. *Photo provided by Phyllis Jordan.*

"Being female was something that played a large role in the strategies I adopted," Phyllis said. Back in the 1970s and 1980s, she had to "insert myself where I was not invited." It also gave her stamina. And vision. She said, "Sometimes the best thing to do is just ignore it when you're being ignored and keep moving forward. Pretend those barriers don't exist and keep doing what you need to get done."

She credits friends and luck for some of her success. In 1978, she became involved in the Specialty Coffee Association of America (as it was then called). Later, she served as its first female president. She met Erna Knutsen at SCAA meetings, and they remained colleagues through Erna's time in the business.

Shelby Westfeldt Mills, the sixth-generation Westfeldt in the coffee importing business, says her idol is Erna Knutsen, who founded

Knutsen Coffees in 1985, after a career as the executive secretary in a Bay Area coffee and spice company. She had been pushed out of the cupping room, since he was a woman. Shelby is aware that Erna said "men gave me a really hard time. They didn't like the idea of women coming in and doing what I'm doing." But she prevailed, and Shelby is proud to follow in her footsteps.

Shelby started at the New York Board of Trade (NYBOT), now the Intercontinental Exchange, where coffee, cocoa and sugar were all traded together as agricultural commodities. "After college I moved to New York. I was on my second interview with a big ad agency when Katrina hit. My dad called, 'We're blind down here. We're moving to North Carolina temporarily, but I need eyes and ears up there. I can get you an internship or clerkship on the NYBOT. I know it's not what you want to do, but can you please do it for just two weeks?' I said of course. I showed up there for what I thought was an interview. I showed up like any good southern girl, in pearls and little kitten heels. Surprise. There was no interview. I was told I was employed and was kept running back and forth all day, in my heels. At the end of the day, I said, 'y'all...which set everyone abuzz: 'Just where are you from?'" Shelby said it did take a little while to get taken seriously among the thousand men and handful of women working there, some of whom were extras in the movie *Trading Places*.

"But I worked hard and learned the trade. At the end of a year, they offered me further training to advance in the company. But I said, 'I love y'all. But you look 20 years older than you are. I love this industry, but I'd rather work for my dad.'" Shelby recalled that when she returned to New Orleans, "I insisted that he interview me, before accepting any position." On January 21, 2007, when she started, it was at the bottom. Not provided with a desk or a computer, Shelby bought her own desk and put it together and brought in her own personal computer. She worked her way up, from the bottom, personal assistant, futures trader, coffee trader, vice president and now president.

She concluded, "Now my dad and I are a good team. And my sister's husband, my brother-in-law Ryan McKinnon is here as well, rounding out the management team."

Janet Dupuy Colley Morse studied sociology and dance at the University of Georgia, not considering a career in coffee and other commodities storage, despite the fact that her great-grandfather, grandfather and her father and his four brothers all worked at Dupuy Storage and Forwarding. She was encouraged in this education choice

Left: Shelby Westfeldt Mills, president, Westfeldt Brothers Coffee Importers; *Right*: Janet Dupuy Colley Morse, vice president of the Dupuy Group. *Photos by David Feldman.*

by her father, a former philosophy major, who believed the liberal arts and fine arts were important.

After Janet decided that "being a professional dancer was not in my stars," she thought she'd give working at Dupuy a try. "And," she said, "fourteen years later, I'm still here." She fell in love with the business because as she sees it, "The most important thing in this business is personal relationships." In fact, she is grateful that she started out in customer service, "answering the phone and helping customers with questions and challenges." She claimed it was "the best education I could get about our business shy of driving a forklift." She can name dozens of people in the city and throughout the country she has become friends with in her years at Dupuy. And those years do not count the time she was hanging out at Dupuy when she was a self-described "rug rat." Now her children come in on weekends and "run around like I used to." Only her preschool-age son gets a special treat: sitting on the forklift, wearing his own hard hat.

A Rich History

Symbol	Last	Change	Open	High	Low	Volume	Settle	Open Int
KCH19	112.30s	-1.60	114.00	115.15	111.90	19053	112.30	116489
KCK19	115.15s	-1.55	116.80	117.95	114.75	7034	115.15	50378
KCN19	117.80s	-1.55	119.40	120.55	117.45	2550	117.80	31858
KCU19	120.35s	-1.55	121.90	123.05	120.00	1168	120.35	14092
KCZ19	123.95s	-1.55	125.60	126.40	123.65	811	123.95	11244
KCH20	127.50s	-1.55	129.05	129.90	127.20	279	127.50	5067
_S_SP_KC	-3.80	unch	-3.90	-3.80	-3.90	11	-3.80	—
RMF19	1609s	-6	1618	1626	1602	6857	1609	41346
RMH19	1625s	-5	1630	1639	1619	4475	1625	33094
[RMH19,	-16							

Coffee futures terminal at Westfeldt Brothers. *Photo by David Feldman.*

One of those long-term relationships is with Shelby Westfeldt Mills, and their connection has an interesting back story: Janet's father, Allan Colley, recalled that that it was Tommy Westfeldt, Shelby's father, who persuaded his own father to get into the computer age. Tommy was walking daily down the street to the exchange to check on the coffee prices written in chalk on a blackboard and reporting back to his father. One day he said, "Dad, by the time I get back here, the prices have changed. We really need a computer." After some persuading that it was a sound investment, Westfeldt Brothers moved into the computer age, which was threatened by Hurricane Katrina, bringing Shelby into the business with her old friend Janet.

BIBLIOGRAPHY

Books

Allen, Stewart Lee. *The Devil's Cup: A History of the World According to Coffee.* New York: Penguin Random House, 1999.

Alvarez, Eugene. *Travel on Southern Antebellum Railroads, 1828–1860.* Tuscaloosa: University of Alabama Press, 1974.

Arceneaux, Pamela D. *Guidebooks to Sin: The Blue Books of Storyville, New Orleans.* New Orleans: Historic New Orleans Collection, 2017.

Arthur, Stanley Clisby. *Old New Orleans; A History of the Vieux Carré, Its Ancient and Historical Buildings.* New Orleans: Harmanson, 1936.

Asbury, Herbert. *The French Quarter: An Informal History of the New Orleans Underworld.* New York: Basic Books, 1958.

Aubertin, Potter. *Oxford Coffee Houses, 1651–1800.* Oxford, UK: Hampden Press, 1987.

Bégué, Elizabeth Kettenring Dutrey. *Mme. Bégué's Recipes of Old New Orleans Creole Cookery.* Gretna, LA: Pelican Publishing Company, 2013.

Brennan, Ella, and Ti Adelaide Martin. *Miss Ella of Commander's Palace.* Layton, UT: Gibbs Smith, 2016.

Bucholz, R.O. *London: A Social and Cultural History, 1550–1750.* New York: Cambridge University Press, 2012.

Campanella, Richard. *Bienville's Dilemma: A Historical Geography of New Orleans.* Lafayette: University of Louisiana at Lafayette Press, 2008.

———. *Lincoln in New Orleans: The 1828–1831 Flatboat Voyages and Their Place in History.* Lafayette: University of Louisiana at Lafayette Press, 2010.

Capella, Anthony. *The Various Flavors of Coffee.* New York: Bantam Books, 2008.

Cassady, Charles, Jr. *Crescent City Crimes: Old New Orleans 1718–1918.* London: Schiffer Publishing, 2017.

Chapman, Garry. *World Commodities: Coffee.* Mankato, MN: Smart Apple Media, 2010.

Bibliography

Cohen, H.A. *Cohen's New Orleans Directory Including Jefferson City, Gretna, Carrollton, Algiers, and McDonogh.* New Orleans: Office of the Picayune, 1855. https://play.google.com/books/reader?id=a7hIAQAAMAAJ&printsec=frontcover&pg=GBS.PR1.

Cole, Catharine. *The Story of the Old French Market New Orleans.* New Orleans: New Orleans Coffee Company, 1916.

Collier, Alexandra "Riki." *Phillip Collier's Making New Orleans: Products Past and Present.* New Orleans: Philbeau Publishing, 2013.

Covey, Herbert C. *What the Slaves Ate: Recollections of African American Foods and Foodways from the Slave Narratives.* Santa Barbara, CA: Greenwood Press/ABC-CLIO, 2009.

Cowan, Brian William. *The Social Life of Coffee: The Emergence of the British Coffeehouse.* New Haven, CT: Yale University Press, 2005.

Dawdy, Shannon Lee. *Building the Devil's Empire: French Colonial New Orleans.* Chicago: University of Chicago Press, 2008.

Ellis, Aytoun. *The Penny Universities: A History of the Coffee-Houses.* London: Secker & Warburg, 1956.

Ellis, Markman. *Eighteenth Century Coffee-House Culture.* London: Pickering & Chatto, 2006.

Ellis, Scott. *Madame Vieux Carré: The French Quarter in the Twentieth Century.* Jackson: University Press of Mississippi, 2010.

Engelhardt, George W. *New Orleans, Louisiana, the Crescent City: The Book of the Picayune Also of the Public Bodies and Business Interests of the Place.* New Orleans: Geo. W. Engelhardt, 1903–4.

Fell, Todd, and April Fell. *250 Years of Creole Cooking.* New Orleans: Gris Gris Publications, 2015.

Frasier, Jim. *The Garden District of New Orleans.* Jackson: University Press of Mississippi, 2012.

Freiberg, Edna B. *Bayou St. John in Colonial Louisiana, 1699–1803.* New Orleans: Freiberg, 1980.

Garvey, Joan, and Mary Louise Widmer. *Beautiful Crescent: A History of New Orleans.* Gretna, LA: Pelican Publishing, 2014.

Gehman, Mary. *Women and New Orleans: A History.* New Orleans: Margaret Media, 1988.

Guenin-Lelle, Dianne. *The Story of French New Orleans: History of a Creole City.* Jackson: University Press of Mississippi, 2016.

Guilbeau, James. *The St. Charles Streetcar: Or the History of the New Orleans & Carrollton Rail Road.* New Orleans: Louisiana Landmarks Society, 1992.

Hattox, Ralph S. *Coffee and Coffeehouses: The Origins of a Social Beverage in the Medieval Near East.* Seattle: University of Washington Press, 1985.

Hirsch, Arnold R., and Joseph Logsdon, eds. Creole New Orleans: *Race and Americanization.* Baton Rouge: Louisiana State University Press, 1992.

Huber, Leonard V. *New Orleans: A Pictorial History.* Gretna, LA: Pelican Publishing, 1991.

Hunter, Louis C. *Steamboats on the Western Rivers: An Economic and Technological History.* Newburyport, MA: Dover Publications, 2012.

Bibliography

Kiple, Kenneth F., and Kriemhild Coneè-Ornelas. *The Cambridge World History of Food*. Cambridge, UK: Cambridge University Press, 2000.

Koehler, Jeff. *Where the Wild Coffee Grows: The Untold Story of Coffee, From the Cloud Forests of Ethiopia to Your Cup*. New York: Bloomsbury, 2017.

Krist, Gary. *Empire of Sin: A Story of Sex, Jazz, Murder, and the Battle for Modern New Orleans*. New York: Broadway Books, 2014.

Laborde, Errol, and Peggy Laborde. *New Orleans: The First 300 Years*. Gretna, LA: Pelican Publishing, 2017.

Laborde, Peggy Scott, and Tom Fitzmorris. *Lost Restaurants of New Orleans and the Recipes that Made Them Famous*. Gretna, LA: Pelican Publishing, 2011.

Leavitt, Mel. *A Short History of New Orleans*. San Francisco: Lexicos. 1982.

Long, Edith Elliott. *Along the Banquette: French Quarter Buildings and Their Stories*. New Orleans: Vieux Carré Property Owners, Residents & Associates Inc., 2004.

Luzianne Coffee Company. *Beyond Cream and Sugar: Recipes to Try with Luzianne Coffee and Chicory*. New Orleans: Reily Foods.

McKinney, Louise. *New Orleans: A Cultural History*. Oxford, UK: Oxford University Press, 2006.

Meister, Erin. *New York City Coffee: A Caffeinated History*. Charleston, SC: The History Press, 2017.

Merrill, Ellen C. *Germans of Louisiana*. Gretna, LA: Pelican Publishing Company, 2014.

Morton, Frederic. *Thunder at Twilight: Vienna 1913–1914*. New York: Macmillan Publishing, 1989.

Murphy, Michael. *Eat Dat New Orleans: A Guide to the Unique Food Culture of the Crescent City*. New York: Countryman Press, 2015.

Nau, John Frederick. *The German People of New Orleans, 1850–1900*. Leiden, NLD: E.J. Brill, 1958.

Norris, William C. *Down in New Orleans: True Stories of a Fabled City*. New Orleans: self-published, 2015.

Parker, Scott F., and Michael W. Austen. *Coffee: Philosophy for Everyone, Grounds for Debate*. New York: John Wiley and Sons, 2011.

Peña, Christopher G. *The Strange Case of Dr. Etienne Deschamps: Murder in the New Orleans French Quarter*. Gretna, LA: Pelican Publishing, 2017.

Pendergrast, Mark. *Uncommon Grounds: The History of Coffee and How It Transformed Our World*. New York: Basic Books, 2010.

Picard, Liza. *Dr. Johnson's London: Coffee-Houses and Climbing Boys, Medicine, Toothpaste and Gin, Poverty and Press-Gangs, Freakshows and Female Education*. New York: St. Martin's Press, 2001.

The Picayune's Creole Cook Book. Kansas City, MO: Andrews McMeel Publishing, 2013.

Postl, Karl. *Americans As They Are, Described in a Tour Through the Valley of the Mississippi*. London: Hurst, Chance and Company, 1828.

Powell, Lawrence N. *The Accidental City: Improvising New Orleans*. Cambridge, MA: Harvard University Press, 2013.

Pruyn, Cassie. *Bayou St. John: A Brief History*. Charleston, SC: The History Press, 2017.

Bibliography

Reed, John Shelton. *Dixie Bohemia: A French Quarter Circle in the 1920s*. Baton Rouge: Louisiana State University Press, 2012.

Reed, Merle. *New Orleans and the Railroads: The Struggle for Commercial Empire, 1830–1860*. Baton Rouge: Louisiana State University Press, 1966.

Ripley, Eliza. *Social Life in Old New Orleans*. Gretna, LA: Pelican Publishing, 1998.

Satin, Morton. *Coffee Talk: The Stimulating Story of the World's Most Popular Brew*. Amherst, NY: Prometheus Books, 2011.

Saurage, H. Norman, III. *The Community Coffee Story*. Baton Rouge, LA: Community Coffee Company, 2014.

Saxon, Lyle. *Fabulous New Orleans*. Gretna, LA: Pelican Publishing, 1988.

Saxon, Lyle, Edward Dreyer and Robert Tallant. *Gumbo Ya-Ya: Folk Tales of Louisiana*. Gretna: Louisiana Publishing Company, 2015.

Schafer, Judith Kelleher. *Slavery, the Civil Law, and the Supreme Court of Louisiana*. Baton Rouge: Louisiana State University Press, 1994.

Schultz, Howard, and Joanne Gordon. *How Starbucks Fought for Its Life Without Losing Its Soul*. New York: Penguin Random House, 2012.

Simmons, P.L. *Coffee and Chicory: Their Culture, Chemical Composition, Preparation for Market, and Consumption, with Simple Tests for Detecting Adulteration, and Practical Hints for the Producer and Consumer*. London: E. & F.N. Spon, 16, Bucklersbury, 1864.

Simms, George A. *Notable Men of New Orleans, 1905*. New Orleans: George Advertising Simms Company, 1906.

Smith, Thomas Ruys. *Southern Queen: New Orleans in the Nineteenth Century*. New York: Continuum Books, 2011.

Sparks, William Henry. *The Memories of Fifty Years: Containing Brief Biographical Notices of Distinguished Americans, and Anecdotes of Remarkable Men; Interspersed with Scenes and Incidents Occuring [sic] During a Long Life of Observation Chiefly Spent in the Southwest*. Philadelphia: Claxton, Remsen and Haffelfinger, 1870.

Spary, E.C. *Eating the Enlightenment: Food and the Sciences in Paris, 1670–1760*. Chicago: University of Chicago, 2012.

Stall, Gaspar J. Proud. *Peculiar New Orleans: The Inside Story*. Baton Rouge, LA: Claiter's Publishing Division, 1984.

Standage, Tom. *A History of the World in 6 Glasses*. New York: Walker & Company, 2005.

Starr, S. Frederick. *Inventing New Orleans: Writings of Lafcadio Hearn*. Jackson: University of Mississippi Press, 2001.

———. *Southern Comfort: The Garden District of New Orleans*. New York: Princeton Architectural Press, 1998.

Sublette, Ned. *The World that Made New Orleans: From Spanish Silver to Congo Square*. Chicago: Lawrence Hill Books, 2008.

Taylor, Troy. *Wicked New Orleans: The Dark Side of the Big Easy*. Charleston, SC: The History Press, 2010.

Thurber, Francis B. *Coffee: From Plantation to Cup, A Brief History of Coffee Production and Consumption*. New York: American Grocer Publishing Association, 1881.

Toledano, Roulhac. *The National Trust Guide to New Orleans: The Definitive Guide to Architectural and Cultural Treasures*. New York: John Wiley & Sons, 1996.

Bibliography

Tucker, Catherine M. *Coffee Culture: Local Experiences, Global Connections.* New York: Routledge, 2011.

Tucker, Susan, ed. *New Orleans Cuisine: Fourteen Signature Dishes and Their Histories.* Jackson: University Press of Mississippi, 2009.

Twain, Mark. *Life on the Mississippi.* New York: Penguin Random House, 2009.

Tyler, Pamela. *Silk Stockings & Ballot Boxes: Women and Politics in New Orleans, 1920–1965.* Athens: University of Georgia Press, 2009.

Ukers, William. *The Romance of Coffee: An Outline History of Coffee and Coffee Drinking Through a Thousand Years.* New York: Tea and Coffee Trade Journal Company, 1948.

Vella, Christina. *Intimate Enemies: The Two Worlds of the Baroness de Pontalba.* Baton Rouge: Louisiana State University Press, 1997.

Vujnovich, Milos M. *Yugoslavs in New Orleans.* Gretna, LA: Firebird Press, 2000.

Wallach, Jennifer Jensen. *How America Eats: A Social History of US Food and Culture.* Lanham, MD: Rowman & Littlefield, 2013.

Weddle, Jeff. *Bohemian New Orleans: The Story of the Outsider and Loujon Press.* Jackson: University Press of Mississippi, 2007.

Weinberg, Bennett Alan. *The World of Caffeine: The Science and Culture of the World's Most Popular Drug.* New York: Routledge, 2001.

Widmer, Mary Lou. *New Orleans in the Forties.* Gretna, LA: Pelican Publishing, 1990.

———. *New Orleans in the Thirties.* Gretna, LA: Pelican Publishing, 1989.

———. *New Orleans 1900–1920.* Gretna: Pelican Publishing, 2007.

Wild, Antony. *Coffee: A Dark History.* New York: W.W. Norton & Company, 2005.

Wilds, John. *James W. Porch and the Port of New Orleans.* New Orleans: James Porch Schwartz, 1984.

Williams, Elizabeth. *New Orleans: A Food Biography.* Lanham, MD: AltaMira Press, 2013.

Wilson, Bee. *Swindled: From Poisoned Sweets to Counterfeit Coffee—The Dark History of the Food Cheats.* London: John Murray, 2009.

Wilson, Nancy Tregere. *Mémerè's Country Creole Cookbook: Recipes and Memories from Louisiana's German Coast.* Baton Rouge: Louisiana State University Press, 2018.

Wright, Charles. *A History of Lloyd's, From the Founding of Lloyd's Coffee House to the Present Day.* London: Macmillan and Company, 1928.

Journals and Magazines

Fortier, Alcée. "The French Language in Louisiana and the Negro-French Dialect." *Transactions of the Modern Language Association of America* 1 (1884): 96–111. doi:10.2307/456001.

McKinney, Louise. "House of Brews: New Orleans' Coffee Culture." *New Orleans Magazine,* September 1995.

Robinson, Malcolm. "Coffee." *New Orleans Official Publication of the Chamber of Commerce of the New Orleans Area,* March 1967.

BIBLIOGRAPHY

Online Books, Journals and Magazines

Belonsky, Andrew. "Truman Capote's Mardi Gras Mommy Issues." *Out*, June 13, 2013. https://www.out.com/travel-nightlife/city-guides/new-orleans/2013/06/03/truman-capotes-mardi-gras-mommy-issues.

Brones, Anna. "Why Is Coffee in France So Bad?" *Slate*, January 24, 2014. https://slate.com/news-and-politics/2014/01/coffee-in-france-is-terrible-why-cant-the-french-brew-a-good-cup-of-coffee.html.

Brown, Nick. "Remembering Specialty Coffee Legend Erna Knutsen." Daily Coffee News by *Roast* magazine, July 16, 2018. https://dailycoffeenews.com/2018/07/16/remembering-specialty-coffee-legend-erna-knutsen.

Coffee and Tea Industries and the Flavor Field 37, Simmons' Spice Mill, New York December 1914. https://books.google.com/books?id=5B0xAQAAMAAJ&pg=RA1-PA1324&lpg=RA1-PA1324&dq=%22stonewall+jackson%22+coffee+new+orleans&source=bl&ots=N5b6DxfwO4&sig=EyLVV9rUIneWvDglFukp4Br75xo&hl=en&sa=X&ved=2ahUKEwjU2-fGrrjcAhUGM6wKHYnxARwQ6AEwDXoECAMQAQ#v=onepage&q=%22stonewall%20jackson%22%20coffee%20new%20orleans&f=false.

Cooper, Anne. "Cowboy Coffee: Horned and Barefooted." *True West*, July 1, 2001. https://truewestmagazine.com/cowboy-coffee.

De Bow, J.D.B., ed. *De Bow's Review and Industrial Resources, Statistics, Etc.* New Orleans, 1853. https://play.google.com/books/reader?id=eCQoAAAAYAAJ&printsec=frontcover&output=reader&hl=en&pg=GBS.PR1.

Eschner, Kat. "The Seventeenth Century 'Women's Petition Against Coffee' Probably Wasn't About Women, or Coffee." *Smithsonian*, October 2, 2017. https://www.smithsonianmag.com/smart-news/meet-pro-temperance-women-who-crusaded-against-coffee-180965039.

Forte, Wesley E. "The Food and Drug Administration and the Economic Adulteration of Food." *Indiana Law Journal* 41, no. 3, article 2. https://www.repository.law.indiana.edu/cgi/viewcontent.cgi?article=3634&context=ilj.

Glover, Ellye Howell. "At Madam Begue's." *Good Housekeeping* (January 1905): 17–19. https://books.google.com/books?id=7Nc-AQAAMAAJ&pg=PA18&lpg=PA18&dq=%22Madame+begue%22+coffee&source=bl&ots=h0cFe3e8pt&sig=qKLN5hHoUKsDZj475PxM5E8AZgc&hl=en&sa=X&ved=0ahUKEwis4_CA5YDcAhVNLKwKHcpZCvAQ6AEIbTAJ#v=onepage&q=%22Madame%20begue%22%20coffee&f=false.

Kaye, Alan S. "The Etymology of 'Coffee': The Dark Brew." *Journal of the American Oriental Society* 106, no. 3 (July–September, 1986): 557–58. https://www.jstor.org/stable/602112.

Kendall, John Smith. *History of New Orleans*. Chicago: Lewis Publishing, 1922. http://penelope.uchicago.edu/Thayer/E/Gazetteer/Places/America/United_States/Louisiana/New_Orleans/_Texts/KENHNO/46*.html.

"The King Cake Has a Queen...And She's Jewish." *Jewish Week*. February 17, 2015. https://jwfoodandwine.com/article/2015/02/17/king-cake-has-queen-and-shes-jewish.

Bibliography

Laborde, Errol. "The Social Significance of the Morning Call." *New Orleans* magazine, December 2012. http://www.myneworleans.com/New-Orleans-Magazine/December-2012/The-Social-Significance-of-the-New-Morning-Call.

Skeie, Trish R. (Rothgeb). "Norway and Coffee." *Flame Keeper*, newsletter of the Roasters Guild, Spring 2003. http://web.archive.org/web/20031011091223/http://roastersguild.org/052003_norway.html.

Smith, K. Annabelle. "The History of the Chicory Coffee Mix That New Orleans Made its Own." *Smithsonian*, March 5, 2014. https://www.smithsonianmag.com/arts-culture/chicory-coffee-mix-new-orleans-made-own-comes-180949950/#l23DfJpMhXGOE5C.99.

Tea and Coffee Trade Journal 42–43 (November 1922). https://books.google.com/books?id=re441wSUkaEC&pg=RA2-PA652&lpg=RA2-PA652&dq=Cottraux+coffee+new+orleans&source=bl&ots=HhpOe751xH&sig=FCI5Z4DIS5ID8m4nRV-GMQz-e60&hl=en&sa=X&ved=0ahUKEwiGw4Dvk6_bAhVHF6wKHSc7CKMQ6AEIiQEwBg#v=onepage&q=Cottraux%20coffee%20new%20orleans&f=false.

Tooker, Poppy. "The Mother of All Iced Coffee." *Biz New Orleans*, July 2018. http://www.bizneworleans.com/Biz-The-Magazine/July-2018/The-Mother-of-All-Iced-Coffee.

Trimble, Marshall. "Arbuckle's Coffee." *True West*, May 18, 2015. Accessed at https://truewestmagazine.com/arbuckles-coffee.

Ukers, William. *All About Coffee*. Project Gutenberg Ebook: April 4, 2009 [EBook #28500]. First copyright 1922.

———. "For the Coffee Convention." *Tea and Coffee Trade Journal* 43 (January 1922). Accessed at https://play.google.com/books/reader?id=re441wSUkaEC&printsec=frontcover&output=reader&hl=en&pg=GBS.PA75.

Van Oss, Salomon Frederik. *American Railroads and British Investors*. London: Effingham Wilson & Company, Royal Exchange, 1893. https://play.google.com/books/reader?id=XjMJAQAAIAAJ&printsec=frontcover&output=reader&hl=en&pg=GBS.PP5.

"What Is the Coffee Ceremony?" *Saveur*, October 20, 2015. http://whatisthecoffeeceremony.com/coffee_ceremony.html.

Websites

American Rails. "Railroads in the 1850s, A Blossoming Industry." https://www.american-rails.com/1850s.html.

Ancestry. "Major US Immigration Ports." https://www.ancestrycdn.com/support/us/2016/11/majorusports.pdf.

Annmarie Skin Care. "Ditch the Chemicals—Seven Ways to Color Your Hair Naturally." https://www.annmariegianni.com/7-ways-to-color-your-hair-naturally.

Aran, Susan. "Paris Is Brewing: The History of Coffee in France Since Louis XIV." *Bonjour Paris: An Insiders Guide*, April 26, 2016. https://bonjourparis.com/food-and-drink/paris-brewing-history-coffee-since-time-louis-xiv.

Bibliography

Baughn, James. "A Visit to the Mississippi River Headwaters (Or Close Enough)." *Southeast Missourian*. October 24, 2017. https://www.semissourian.com/blogs/pavementends/entry/70188.

Beauregard Keyes House. "The Beauregard Keyes House and Garden Museum." http://www.bkhouse.org/learn.

Blackout Coffee Company. "The Three Waves of Coffee." August 19, 2013. https://www.blackoutcoffee.com/blogs/the-reading-room/the-three-waves-of-coffee.

Blotnick, Emmy. "Five Historical Attempts to Ban Coffee." Mental Floss. December 4, 2013. http://mentalfloss.com/article/12662/5-historical-attempts-ban-coffee.

Brewing Coffee Manually. "Chicory: History, Blending, and New Orleans Style Coffee." February 22, 2015. http://www.manualcoffeebrewing.com/chicory-history-blending-and-new-orleans-style-coffee.

Brister, Nancy. "The Old Public Markets." Old New Orleans. http://old-new-orleans.com/NO_Markets.

Brown, Nick. "A Brief History of Global Coffee Production As We Know It (1963–2013)." Daily Coffee News. https://dailycoffeenews.com/2014/07/17/a-brief-history-of-global-coffee-production-as-we-know-it-1963-2013.

Bureau of Alcohol, Tobacco, Firearms and Explosives. "Isadore 'Izzie' Einstein." https://www.atf.gov/our-history/isador-izzy-einstein.

Caffé Florian. "From Triumphant Venice to the Present." https://www.caffeflorian.com/en/heritage/venice-triumphantto-present.html.

Castner, Charles B. "A Brief History of The Louisville & Nashville Railroad." Louisville & Nashville Railroad Historical Society. http://www.lnrr.org/History.aspx.

Chamberlain, Gaius. "Norbert Rillieux." Black Inventor Online Museum. November 26, 2012. http://blackinventor.com/norbert-rillieux.

Cho, Nicholas. "The BGA and the Third Wave." CoffeeGee. April 1, 2005. http://coffeegeek.com/opinions/bgafiles/04-02-2005.

City of Vienna. "History of Viennese Coffee House Culture." https://www.wien.gv.at/english/culture-history/viennese-coffee-culture.htm.

Coffeechemistry.com. "Chemical Changes in Coffee During Roasting." April 27, 2015. https://www.coffeechemistry.com/quality/roasting/chemical-changes-during-roasting.

Coffee Merchant. "Coffee Encyclopedia." http://www.supremo.be/en/continent/coffee-encyclopedia.

Coffee Research. "Coffee Roasting." http://www.coffeeresearch.org/coffee/roasting.htm.

Condon, Joseph. "Climbing the Branches of My Family Tree: Friday's Famous—Francois Gabriel 'Valcour' Aime (1797–1867)." August 17, 2012. http://climbingthebranches.blogspot.com/2012/08/fridays-famous-francois-gabriel-valcour.html.

Corbertt, Bob. "List of English Language Books and Articles Relevant to Vienna Coffee Houses." Webster University. http://faculty.webster.edu/corbetre/philosophy/vienna/books-coffee.html.

Bibliography

Dooky Chase Restaurant. "About the Chef." https://www.dookychaserestaurant.com/about/chef.

Ferguson, Mike. "Remembering Erna Knutsen, Coffee's Feminist Pioneer." Sprudge. August 6, 2018. https://sprudge.com/remembering-erna-knutsen-coffees-feminist-pioneer-135417.html.

Freeman School of Business–Tulane University. "William B. Burkenroad Jr." July 1, 2014. https://freemancentennial.tulane.edu/2014/07/01/william-b-burkenroad-jr.

Gillie's Coffee. "Meet Donald Schoenholt." https://www.gilliescoffee.com/coffee-man/Schoenholt, Donald.

Gold, Jonathan. "La Mill: The Latest Buzz." *LA Weekly*. March 12, 2008. https://www.laweekly.com/restaurants/la-mill-the-latest-buzz-2152451.

Grant, Bonnie L. "Information on How to Grow Chicory." Gardening Knowhow. https://www.gardeningknowhow.com/edible/herbs/chicory/growing-chicory.htm.

Hémard, Ned. "Beignet...Done That!" New Orleans Nostalgia http://www.neworleansbar.org/uploads/files/Beignet%20Done%20That%20Article_4-3.pdf.

———. "Coffee with Chicory." New Orleans Nostalgia. http://www.neworleansbar.org/uploads/files/Coffee%20With%20Chicory%2012_3_18.pdf.

———. "A Multifacted Gem." New Orleans Nostalgia. http://www.neworleansbar.org/uploads/files/A%20Multifaceted%20Gem2_6-18.pdf.

Iyer, Praba. "'N Dive into Chicory." India Currents. February 14, 2017. https://indiacurrents.com/n-dive-chicory.

John Carter Brown Library. "Remember Haiti: Economy." http://www.brown.edu/Facilities/John_Carter_Brown_Library/exhibitions/remember_haiti/economy.php.

Knapp, Gwendolyn. "Pralines Are More Than Just New Orleans' Signature Candy: How Generations of Black Women Crafted a Livelihood from Sugar, Milk, Butter, and Pecans." *Eater*. October 27, 2016. https://www.eater.com/2016/10/27/13422426/praline-new-orleans-pecan-candy.

Laudan, Rachel. "Beignets and Luqam: Thoughts from Cathy Kaufman." July 6, 2009. http://www.rachellaudan.com/2009/07/beignets-and-luqam-thoughts-from-cathy-kaufman.html.

Louisiana: Feed Your Soul. "Louisiana State Museum Online Exhibits: The Cabildo: Two Centuries Of Louisiana History: Antebellum Louisiana III: Urban Life." https://www.crt.state.la.us/louisiana-state-museum/online-exhibits/the-cabildo/antebellum-louisiana-urban-life/index.

———. "Louisiana State Museum Online Exhibits: Coffee Trade and the Port of New Orleans." https://www.crt.state.la.us/louisiana-state-museum/online-exhibits/coffee-trade-and-port-of-new-orleans/j-aron-and-company-the-role-of-the-coffee-importer.

Lowry, Bradford. "The History of First, Second and Third Wave Coffee." Craft Beverage Jobs. https://www.craftbeveragejobs.com/the-history-of-first-second-and-third-wave-coffee-22315.

Bibliography

McGunnigle, Nora. NOLA'S Coffee Culture Grinds on (20 Billion Cups and Counting)." Thrillist. January 26, 2017. https://www.Thrillist.Com/Drink/New-Orleans/New-Orleans-Coffee-Culture.

Media NOLA. "Madame Begue's Restaurant." http://medianola.org/discover/place/863/Madame-Begues-Restaurant.

Meserve, Myles. "The Israels: How This Legendary Family Went from Coffee Trading to Ponzi Scheming." Business Insider. June 28, 2012. https://www.businessinsider.com/the-israel-banking-family-2012-6.

Morris, Jonathan. "The Cappuccino Conquests: The Transnational History of Italian Coffee." University of Hertfordshire. https://www.academia.edu/379110.

Morris, Tyler. "The 19th-Century Swill Milk Scandal that Poisoned Infants with Whiskey Runoff." Atlas Obscura. November 27, 2017. https://www.atlasobscura.com/articles/swill-milk-scandal-new-york-city.

Myhrvold, Nathan. "The Maillard Reaction." Modernist Cuisine Blog, March 20, 2013. https://modernistcuisine.com/2013/03/the-maillard-reaction.

National Coffee Association. "Coffee Around the World." http://www.ncausa.org/About-Coffee/Coffee-Around-the-World.

———. "The History of Coffee." http://www.ncausa.org/About-Coffee/History-of-Coffee.

———. "10 Steps from Seed to Cup." http://www.ncausa.org/about-coffee/10-steps-from-seed-to-cup.

———. Anonymous. "What Is Coffee?" http://www.ncausa.org/About-Coffee/What-is-Coffee.

NOLA.com. "When Smoky Mary Was Queen of the Pontchartrain Railroad." July 14, 2017. https://www.nola.com/300/2017/07/smoky_mary_new_orleans.html.

Orleans Coffee. "What Is Chicory?" https://www.orleanscoffee.com/how_to/what-is-chicory.

Pabari, Suneal. "10 Differences Between Robusta and Arabica Coffee." The Roasters Pack, September 24, 2014. https://theroasterspack.com/blogs/news/15409365-10-differences-between-robusta-arabica-coffee

Platt, R. Eric. "Valcour Aime." 64 Parishes. http://www.knowlouisiana.org/entry/valcour-aime.

Poggioli, Sylvia. "Italy's Coffee Culture Brims with Rituals and Mysterious Rules." NPR Morning Addition, July 14, 2017. https://www.npr.org/sections/thesalt/2017/07/14/535638587/italys-coffee-culture-brims-with-rituals-and-mysterious-rules.

Professor 1130. "The Le Carpentier Family of New Orleans, Louisiana." https://lecarpentieroflouisiana.wordpress.com/2015/03/29/hello-world.

Reinecke, George F. "The National and Cultural Groups of New Orleans." Louisiana Folklife: A Guide to the State. http://www.louisianafolklife.org/lt/virtual_books/guide_to_state/NOGroups.html.

Rhinehart, Ric. "What Is Specialty Coffee?" Specialty Coffee Association of America, 2009. http://scaa.org/?page=RicArtp1.

Bibliography

Richard, Charley. "200 Years of Progress in the Louisiana Sugar Industry: A Brief History." Reprinted from *Sugar Journal* (February 1995). http://www.assct.org/louisiana/History%20Louisiana%20Sugar%20Industry.pdf.

Schoenholt, Donald. Comment. http://www.coffeed.com/viewtopic.php?f=21&t=1768&start=50.

Specialty Coffee Association of America. "A Botanists' Guide to Specialty Coffee." https://sca.coffee/research/botany?page=resources&d=a-botanists-guide-to-specialty-coffee.

Spellen, Suzanne. "King Coffee, the Magic Beans that Powered Brooklyn." Brownstoner. https://www.brownstoner.com/history/brooklyn-history-dumbo-empire-stores-john-arbuckle.

Sprudge. "The Pope Prefers Ristretto, and Other Fun Papal Coffee Facts." April 23, 2013. https://sprudge.com/pope-prefers-ristretto-while-standing-36636.html.

St. James Hotel. "The Legend of the St. James Hotel New Orleans." https://www.saintjameshotel.com/history.

Supremo. "Coffee Glossary." http://www.supremo.be/en/node/7.

Tujague's. "History." http://www.tujaguesrestaurant.com/history.

Turkish Coffee. "Social History of Turkish Coffee." http://www.turkishcoffee.us/articles/history/social-history-of-turkish-coffee.

———. "Turkish Coffee from Mythology to History." http://www.turkishcoffee.us/articles/history/turkish-coffee-from-mythology-to-history.

U.S. Department of Transportation. "The Rambler's History of New Orleans with Thanks to the American Guide Series." https://www.fhwa.dot.gov/infrastructure/neworleansrambler.cfm.

U.S. Food and Drug Administration. "Part I: The 1906 Food and Drugs Act and Its Enforcement." https://www.fda.gov/AboutFDA/History/FOrgsHistory/EvolvingPowers/ucm054819.htm.

Vargas, Paul. "French Market Coffee, New Orleans." https://paulvargas1.wordpress.com/french-market-coffee-new-orleans.

Walker, Andy. "1913: When Hitler, Trotsky, Tito, Freud and Stalin all Lived in the Same Place." Today Programme, BBC Radio, April 18, 2013. https://www.bbc.com/news/magazine-21859771.

Walton, Geri. "Napoleon's Coffee Obsession." Geri Walton Unique Histories from the 18th and 19th Centuries. https://www.geriwalton.com/napoleons-love-of-coffee.

Weizmann Institute of Science. "The Alkaloids." https://www.weizmann.ac.il/plants/aharoni/sites/plants.aharoni/files/uploads/june192007.pdf.

Wikipedia. "Benjamin Henry Latrobe." Accessed June 8, 2018. https://en.wikipedia.org/wiki/Benjamin_Henry_Latrobe.

———. "Köppen Climate Classification." Accessed December 1, 2018. https://en.wikipedia.org/wiki/Köppen_climate_classification#Tropical_monsoon_climate.

———. "Paul Morphy." https://en.wikipedia.org/wiki/Paul_Morphy.

Zaimeche, Salah. "The Coffee Route from Yemen to London 10th–17th Centuries." Muslim Heritage. http://muslimheritage.com/article/coffee-route.

Bibliography

Dissertations

Nunez, Chanda. "Just like Ole' Mammy Used to Make: Reinterpreting New Orleans African-American Praline Vendors as Entrepreneurs." University of New Orleans Theses and Dissertations, 2011. 128. https://scholarworks.uno.edu/td/128.

Newspapers

Daily Delta. February 8, 1850.
Daily Picayune. Advertisement. February 21, 1878, 6.
———. Advertisement. December 7, 1884, 5.
———. January 11, 1843.
———. Advertisement. July 11, 1894, 8.
———. "Christmas Morn at the French Market. The Cosmopolitan Character of the Day's Celebration Seen There." December 26, 1896.
———. "The Killing of Fazio. Prelimary Examination of the Accused, Voutrain, before Recorder Ford—Released On." April 18, 1883.
———. March 12, 1844, 2.
———. "Terrible Steamboat Explosion." November 16, 1849.
———. "Vicksburg. More Cotton than the Roads Can Carry." December 18, 1884, 1.
———. "Women's World and Work Column." March 18, 1894, 28.
Hermann, Peter. "Grounded in Tradition (The Ethiopian Coffee Ceremony)." *Baltimore Sun*, October 4, 2006. http://articles.baltimoresun.com/2006-10-04/news/0610030041_1_ethiopian-coffee-coffee-ceremony-making-coffee.
Karst, James. "A Short History of the Beignet in New Orleans." NOLA.com | *Times-Picayune*. October 17, 2016. https://www.nola.com/dining/index.ssf/2016/10/a_short_history_of_the_beignet.html.
L'Ami des Lois et Journal du Soir (New Orleans, LA). "Court of Probates—Sale by the Register of Wills." March 18, 1818, 4.
Lonsdale, Henry T. "H.T. Lonsdale, Son & Co.'s Weekly Coffee Statement." *Daily Picayune*, December 22, 1860.
Louisiana Advertiser. May 30, 1820, 4.
———. July 25, 1825, 2.
Maloney, Ann. "Coffee and Chicory Cookie Recipe for a Bit of New Orleans Flavor." NOLA.com | *Times-Picayune*. December 21, 2017. https://www.nola.com/food/index.ssf/2017/12/coffee_and_chicory_cookie_reci.html.
Marshall, Carolyn. "Alfred H. Peet, 87, Dies; Leader of a Coffee Revolution." *New York Times*, September 3, 2007. https://www.nytimes.com/2007/09/03/us/03peet.html.
New-Orleans Commercial Bulletin. August 31, 1867, 1.
———. September 12, 1871, 5.
New-Orleans Times. December 30, 1865, 2.
———. October 18, 1866, 2.

Bibliography

Times-Picayune. August 28, 1927, 39.

———. "Dorothy Dix to Address Business Women at Lunch." January 4, 1922, 10.

———. "Movies Filmed in Green Shutter." January 20, 1922.

———. "Mrs. Porter Visits Places Familiar to Story Writer." March 19, 1922, 3.

———. "New Orleans' Vieux Carre Now Coming into Its Own." April 16, 1922, 75.

———. "Opening of Green Shutter." November 27, 1921.

Walker, Judy. "Coffee: The Times-Picayune Covers 175 Years of New Orleans History." NOLA.com | *Times-Picayune.* February 2, 2012. https://www.nola.com/175years/index.ssf/2012/02/coffee_the_times-picayune_cove.html.

Weekly Picayune. "Dealing in Stocks." December 13, 1841.

Interviews

Bob Arceneaux (David Feldman)
Ian Barrilleaux (David Feldman)
Stephen Bauer
Tish Casey
Leah Chase
Allan Colley (with David Feldman)
Jodi Conachen
Sarah Corsiatto
Demian Estevez (with David Feldman)
Rien Fertel
Lauren Fink (David Feldman)
Mary Gehman
Byron Gomez
Eliot Guthrie (David Feldman)
Sarah Lambeth (David Feldman)
Tommy LeBlanc (with David Feldman)
Geoffrey Meeker (with David Feldman)
Jim McCarthy
Jeff McCrory
Shelby Westfeldt Mills
Lauren Morlock (with David Feldman)
Janet Dupuy Colley Morse (with David Feldman)
Kevin Pedeaux
Chaco Rathke (with David Feldman)
Wade Rathke (with David Feldman)
Jacques Roman
Jay Roman IV
Donna M. Saurage
Charlie Schmitz
Tommy Westfeldt
Bobby Winston (David Feldman)

INDEX

A

Aron, J. 88, 89, 91

B

beignet 103, 104, 105, 106, 107, 108, 109, 110, 111, 114, 153
biggin 40, 61, 62
Biggin, Monsieur 62
Bories, Robert 88
brûlot 60, 117
Burkenroad, William B., Jr. 88
Burkenroads 88
Burkenroad, William 88

C

café au lait 57, 58, 102, 103, 105, 106, 107
café brûlot 60, 117
Café Procope 21, 23, 44
Calas 37, 39, 116
Chicoree 68
chicory 13, 39, 59, 65, 66, 67, 68, 69, 70, 71, 72, 91, 93, 95, 103, 107, 116, 117, 119, 133, 139, 153, 156, 157
coffee break 116, 159
Coffee Exchange 44, 45, 48, 49, 50, 51, 52, 57, 116
coffeehouses 20, 21, 22, 23, 44, 45, 46, 48, 49, 50, 51, 53, 54, 57, 60, 76, 90, 92, 93, 101, 102, 104, 115, 116, 117, 118, 121, 129, 130, 133, 135, 154, 155, 167
coffee shop 164

INDEX

Colley, Allen 88, 95, 173
Cottraux, E.P. 88, 103

D

D. Altmau's Coffee House 49
de Bienville 13, 14, 15, 16, 17, 53, 130
de Clieu, Gabriel Mathieu 13, 24
Dupuy 95, 96, 97, 137, 171, 172
Dupuy, John 95, 97
Dutrey's Coffee House 39

E

Elkin's Coffee House 45

F

Fair Grinds Coffee House 155, 156
First Wave 122, 125, 127
First Wavers 121
free lunch 50
French Market 34, 37, 39, 91, 92, 101, 102, 103, 104, 105, 106, 107, 108, 109, 113, 114, 116, 162
French Quarter 114

G

German 16, 17, 18, 21, 31, 34, 39, 54, 59, 62, 66, 68, 73, 85
Germany 39, 66
Globe Coffee House 49
Green Dragon Coffee House 45
Gwathmey's Coffee House 46

H

Hewlett's Coffee House 48
Hewlett's Exchange 45

I

Israel, Leon, Jr. 89
Israel, Leon 88, 89
Israel, Samuel 89

J

Jefferson, Thomas 18, 43, 45, 49, 74

K

Kaldi 19, 20, 162
Knutsen, Erna 126, 133, 170, 171

L

Lloyd's Coffee House 45, 51
Lonsdale, Henry 67, 76, 77, 78, 86, 88, 95

M

Madary, William, III 89, 90
Madary, Matt 89, 90
Merchant's Coffee House 46
Merchant's Exchange 45, 50
Mills, Shelby Westfeldt 78, 88, 170, 171, 172, 173

Index

Mississippi River 13, 14, 51, 73, 74, 78, 106, 113, 130, 157
Morse, Janet Dupuy Colley 95, 172, 173

N

Napoleon 18, 23, 24, 43, 66, 67

O

Orleans Coffee House 49

P

Peet, Alfred 125, 126
Peet's 122, 125, 126, 127
Penny Post Coffee House 117
Penny Universities 23, 44
pralines 37, 38

R

Reily 88, 91, 119
Reily, William, Jr. 91
Reily, William 91
Rillieux 46, 47
roasts 29
Rose 34, 35, 36, 37

S

Saint-Domingue 17, 18, 25, 43, 44, 46
Sazerac Coffee House 51
Second Wave 94, 121, 125, 126
St. Charles Exchange 45
Storyville 54, 114, 130, 143, 145

T

Third Wave 122, 127, 162
Tontine Coffee House 45, 51
Tremoulet's Exchange 45, 48
True Brew Coffee House 155

V

vendeuses 33, 40, 116

W

Westfeldt 78, 79, 81, 88, 96, 97, 148, 172, 173
Westfeldt, George 78, 115
Westfeldt, Kitty Monroe 115
Westfeldt, Martha Gasquet 115
Westfeldt, Tommy 78, 88, 94, 173

ABOUT THE AUTHOR

A history lover, Suzanne has volunteered as a docent at the Smithsonian's National Museum of American History and the New Orleans–based World War II Museum. She is currently a volunteer docent at the Historic New Orleans Collection, a museum, research center and publisher dedicated to preserving the history and culture of New Orleans and the Gulf South. Semi-retired from executive positions in nonprofit organizations, Suzanne works as a tour guide in New Orleans, presenting French Quarter, Garden District, culinary history, cemetery and ghost tours. She has developed two unique tours: Jewish New Orleans and Women of New Orleans. She volunteers as a guide for Friends of the Cabildo and is the 2017 recipient of Friends of the Cabildo's Golden Shoe award. Her previous book is *Volunteering Around the Globe: Life-Changing Travel Adventures*.

www.ingramcontent.com/pod-product-compliance
Lightning Source LLC
Chambersburg PA
CBHW042139160426
43201CB00021B/2341